Delivering Foster Care

Acknowledgements

First and foremost we must acknowledge our debt to the hundreds of foster carers and fostering staff and their managers in all parts of Scotland for their extensive support. Our appreciation also goes to the Association of Directors of Social Work, its Children and Families Committee and its Research Committee for supporting the study. At a time of re-organisation and many other work pressures, the staff of the social work departments were most generous with their time and this is greatly appreciated. The same also goes for all the staff at NFCA Scotland and Dr Barnardo's Scotland.

Many thanks are due to Gerri McAndrew, Executive Director of the NFCA and to Suzette Waterhouse for sharing with us their questionnaire to the agencies and for allowing us to quote extensively from their study on the organisation of fostering services in England. Also to Philip Gregg who shared with us his questionnaire to foster carers. Roy Parker, David Berridge, Harriet Dempster and Lydia Lambert made very helpful suggestions which are greatly appreciated. A number of other individuals read selected parts of the report and offered us invaluable advice. On the more technical side we are grateful to Euan McKay of Glasgow University and Caroline Robinson of the Statslab at Edinburgh University who provided valuable computing and statistical assitance. Finally our warm thanks go to Linda Morris for her secretarial assistance and to Toby Morris for his computing advice especially at times of crisis.

We would also like to express our appreciation to our funders, the Social Work Services Group of the Scottish Office, and the Central Research Unit which provided its social research service to the team.

Note about the authors

John Triseliotis is Emeritus Professor at the University of Edinburgh and visiting Professor and Senior Research Fellow at the University of Strathclyde.

Moira Borland is Research Fellow at the University of Glasgow.

Malcolm Hill is Professor of Social Work at the University of Glasgow.

Delivering Foster Care

John Triseliotis
Moira Borland
Malcolm Hill

B *ritish*
A *gencies*
for **A** *doption*
and **F** *ostering*

Published by
British Agencies for Adoption & Fostering
(BAAF)
Skyline House
200 Union Street
London SE1 0LX

Charity registration 275689

© John Triseliotis, Moira Borland,
Malcolm Hill 2000

**British Library Cataloguing in Publication
Data**
A catalogue record for this book is available
from the British Library

ISBN 1 873868 80 4

Project management by Shaila Shah, Head of
Communications, BAAF
Photographs on cover (posed by models)
by John Birdsall
Designed by Andrew Haig & Associates
Typeset by Avon Dataset Ltd, Bidford on Avon
Printed by Russell Press Ltd. (TU),
Nottingham

Contents

Foreword

Gerri McAndrew
Executive Director, NFCA

Foster care throughout the UK is at a crossroads. In all four countries, plans concerning services to children are being set in place; these will determine the future development of children's services in general and fostering in particular for at least the next ten years. For many young people who need to be looked after by local authorities, foster care offers their best hope of overcoming the disadvantages, which have left them in need of supplemented care. A professional, well-resourced foster care service will help to ensure their safety and protection.

This study, *Delivering Foster Care*, therefore, comes at an opportune time. Although primarily a Scottish study, its findings and emerging key themes are similar to those reflected in the foster care service throughout the UK. Issues of strategic policy, practice, management structures, recruitment and retention, training and clarity of roles and responsibilities require attention if the foster care service is to make more of its present strengths.

That so many carers responded to the questionnaire reflects the potential wealth of expertise and experience that often remains untapped. It is, therefore, particularly encouraging that this study includes carers' views and gives them equal status with that of staff in local authorities. The difference of views between carers and agencies is noticeable. Hopefully their views will be noted and acted upon.

Delivering Foster Care draws on a range of experiences and perceptions, from managers, policy makers, practitioners and carers. It makes excellent recommendations for the future management of the service. If these recommendations are acted upon by those responsible for delivering the service, the foster care service may have a good chance of providing for society's children in the future.

1 Introduction and background to the study

SOME BACKGROUND ISSUES

This book discusses the nature of fostering from the perspectives of foster carers and local authority fostering agencies. It is based on a study which was prompted mainly by concerns about the perceived inadequate supply of foster carers and issues of recruitment and retention. Though the study was set up in Scotland, similar concerns were being voiced in England. For example, the NFCA (1997) reported that foster care was in crisis. Similarly, the House of Commons Health Committee Report (1998, p 31) spoke of 'a developing crisis' in foster care and urged for measures to reverse what it described as 'decades of neglect'.

The research project was set up in 1996 with two key aims:

a) to examine the characteristics, motives, and social circumstances of active and former foster carers; seek explanations concerning their retention and loss; describe the experience of fostering, including contact issues between parents and children; and evaluate post-placement support and general experiences of the fostering service.

b) to identify the policies, structures and organisation of the local authorities with respect to fostering, including: the authorities' fostering needs; recruitment approaches; the preparation, assessment and training of carers; post-placement support to children and carers; the assessment of children and the matching processes followed, as well as the financial arrangements and monitoring mechanisms in place.

The study obtained information by means of self-completion question-naires and interviews from foster carers and senior child care managers in all 32 Scottish local authorities. This book concentrates on reporting the findings, and discussing issues and concepts which have wider relevance to policy makers, managers and practitioners in the UK. Where possible, analogies and contrasts are made with England, drawing mainly on the work of Waterhouse (1997) concerning the organisation and delivery of fostering services in England. This opening chapter briefly reviews current understandings of these services.

The changing nature of fostering

Fostering usually involves the temporary removal of children from their birth families to live with foster carers until their own families are ready to have them back or the children move on to more permanent arrangements. Being separated from parents is a stressful and bewildering experience for the children. Furthermore, they are expected to settle down without over-attaching themselves to their substitute carers in readiness for their return home or for moving on. Not surprisingly, many children identify fostering with 'moving on and on' (Hill *et al*, 1989).

Foster carers themselves are expected not only to provide family care without becoming too attached to the children, but also to deploy high skills and expected to care for some very troubled and troublesome children and young people. These factors have led to what has been termed the "role ambiguity" of foster care, that is, undertaking a broadly parenting role yet being temporary carers (Berridge and Cleaver, 1987).

There is substantial evidence that the children being looked after in foster care now are very different from those of even 25 years ago (Bebbington and Miles, 1989; Triseliotis *et al*, 1995b; Sinclair *et al*, 1995). Most of those looked after in foster care now would have been in residential care 20 years ago, and those in foster care then are now looked after in their own homes. The recent implementation of new Children Acts in England and Wales, Scotland and Northern Ireland, with more stringent conditions under which children may be compulsorily accommodated away from home, is leading to fewer but possibly even more problematic children entering the care system. Many of them can display behavioural and emotional problems; some have offended; others have disabilities, are HIV positive or have been seriously abused.

These developments inevitably make high demands on the knowledge and expertise of fostering staff and of the experience, caring and "treatment" skills of foster carers. To care effectively for this group of children foster carers rely heavily on sharing the task with the fostering services who are expected to equip them with the necessary preparation, continued training and post-placement support. The social work services are continuously faced with the task of organising, managing and staffing the fostering service in a way that will deliver high quality services able to respond to the complex needs of the children, their families and their carers.

Supply and demand

Issues of supply and demand for foster carers have been central to most debates on foster care over many years now. In both Scotland and England foster care is now the main form of substitute care offered to children looked after away from home. Because of the demand for placements, the fostering services rely heavily on a regular supply of foster carers if there is to be any possibility of offering choice to the children and help achieve good matching.

Several studies have indicated a shortage of foster carers with the necessary skills and expertise to take on specific tasks so that social workers are often using the first available placement, with the concept of "matching" going by the wayside (Berridge and Cleaver, 1987; Shaw and Hipgrave, 1989; Triseliotis et al, 1995b; Sinclair et al, 1995). The House of Commons Health Committee Report (1998, p 31) referred to an SSI survey in England which found that for 75 per cent of children there was no choice of placement. A study of Birmingham's child care services revealed that foster placements were difficult to find for even very young children and that fostering for those over ten was almost non-existent (Coffin, 1993). Hence often children are placed with carers who are either far away from the children's families and/or whose skills do not always match with the children's needs, especially in the case of adolescents (Triseliotis et al, 1995b).

Recruitment difficulties have also been reported in relation to placements for minority ethnic children. It has been suggested that the presence of staff from minority ethnic backgrounds enhances recruitment of carers from similar ethnic backgrounds. There have been particular shortages of Asian carers (Shaw and Hipgrave, 1989; Lowe, 1990; Caesar et al, 1994; Berridge, 1997). There is no single reason for why more people do not come forward to foster. Explanations vary from low allowances/pay (Campbell and Whitelaw-Downs, 1987) to the increase in the proportion of women who find out of home employment more attractive (Parker, 1978).

The characteristics of foster carers

Before the present study, the most comprehensive picture of the characteristics of foster carers remained that of Gray and Parr in 1957 in England and Wales. There have been two more recent studies with more limited objectives by Bebbington and Miles (1990) and Ames (1993). The latter studies concluded that foster carers constituted more of a microcosm of wider society than previously. Based on a survey of 13 local authorities in England, Bebbington and Miles (1990) singled out certain continuing distinguishing features that, as a group, foster carers tend to share:

- being slightly older on average than all parents with dependent children;
- only one in eight having a child under five;
- being two parent households; and
- having a slightly larger family size and bigger homes.

Motivation to foster

Recruitment is inevitably linked to motivation, awareness about need, and information about the children needing families. Personal, family or social factors and circumstances also appear to play a big part in the decision. Fostering has often been seen as a form of altruism and/or 'an inclination to goodness'. Though both these qualities have been puzzling not only to students of foster care, but also to philosophers, theologians and others through the centuries, there is no agreement as to their source. A twist to the debate is the assertion, according to psychoanalytic theory, that many of our actions are motivated by unconscious forces and are therefore unknown to us.

Prosser (1978), in her review of foster care research, subscribes to the idea of unconscious motives and urges social workers to "delve" deeply during their selection of foster carers. Rowe et al (1984) found that many foster carers have a wish to help underprivileged children together with a desire for one or more additional children in their family. Dando and Minty (1987) claimed from their study that there were two motivations which brought carers into fostering:

- a desire to parent a child, where a couple were unable to conceive; and
- an identification with deprived and unhappy children as a result of past experience during childhood.

The same researchers add that foster carers who apparently claimed to act from motives of social concern and altruism 'were also seen by fostering officers to have demonstrated a real ability to foster' (Dando and Minty, 1987, p 389).

The ascription of many actions to the unconscious has possibly contributed to the over-attention paid in the fostering and adoption literature of the past on so called "unhealthy" and "pathological" rather than "healthy" motives (see Fanshel, 1966). Motives were often examined in an attempt to identify the so-called "pathogenic" factors behind them and applicants were treated as suspects. More recently, the individual and group methods introduced for the family assessment or home study and preparation of applicant(s) have shifted the process to a more task-centred and educative approach (See Triseliotis, 1988 and Triseliotis *et al*, 1995a). This does not mean that assessment can be any less rigorous.

Recruitment and the retention of foster carers
There has been no systematic British study of why some carers continue and others cease to foster. Recent figures produced by an NFCA survey of local authorities in England suggest that around eight per cent of carers leave the service each year (Waterhouse, 1997). A study that took place some 20 years ago in a single agency in England suggested that the losses of foster carers then were so high (around 27 per cent annually) that, if departments could hold on to their existing carers, there would be almost no need for new recruits (Jones, 1975). Many of the explanations offered for these losses had to do with the operation of the fostering service.

Bebbington and Miles (1990) reported that hundreds of families were giving up fostering each year 'because they felt undervalued and unsupported', but specific figures were lacking (p 301). An account of child care strategies in Birmingham (Caesar *et al*, 1994) stated that foster carers complained of lack of recognition, low status, inadequate training and support, and children remaining too long in short-term placements without an allocated social worker.

Sellick (1992) and Berridge (1997) also refer to the 'low' status ascribed to foster carers within social services departments and attribute this to the fact that, in the past, foster carers have been seen as substitute parents and that this form of work does not require special skills. More positive methods suggested for retaining carers include: quick response to requests for help with difficulties; better training and help in the management of behaviours; and increased levels of support, including arrangements for breaks and respite (see Berridge, 1997).

Some studies link recruitment and retention with levels of pay (Campbell and Whitelaw-Downs 1987; Chamberlain *et al*, 1992). It is well known that local authorities have a variety of pay schemes and significant differences can exist both between neighbouring authorities and within authorities for caring for similar children (Bebbington and Miles 1990; Lowe, 1990). Each of the eight Welsh authorities studied by Pithouse *et al* (1994) was reported to be paying foster carers below National Foster Care Association recommended rates.

Foster care outcomes

A brief overview of foster care outcome studies over the last 30 or so years suggests that many children benefit from family foster care. Much depends on the type of placement and its aims and the way outcomes are measured and at which stage. Success has often been measured by the absence of breakdown in the placement, though nowadays more than one measure is likely to be used for making outcome judgements. Minni's (1999) recent study showed that the self-esteem of children who went into foster care improved over a nine month period.

Short-term placements, that is, those meant to last for up to about three months, have been found to be far more successful than those meant to last for over two years. The exact proportion is unclear. Taking everything into account, an average breakdown rate of 30 per cent in the first two years for all age-groups and types of placements can be expected (see Triseliotis, 1989; Berridge, 1997; Sellick and Thoburn, 1996). Rowe *et al* (1989), using more sophisticated measures, but relying on the judgements of social workers, found from their survey that when all ages and types of placement were taken together, just half were said to have lasted as planned over the three year period.

Placements become more vulnerable to breakdown with the children's increased age and increased behavioural or emotional difficulties. By adolescence, the attrition rate can be as high as 60 per cent (Strathclyde study, 1991; Triseliotis *et al*, 1995b). However, those children whose placements stabilise can benefit considerably. Some teenagers can be provided with a social base which has mostly been absent from their past lives. It is conjectured that outcomes are affected by the amount of social work support provided to carers (Sellick and Thoburn, 1996) and by the quality of direct work with children carried out by social workers to help them manage their behaviour within care, with the emotional stresses of rejection, separation and loss. The studies summarised in the Department of Health's report (1985) and Cleaver's summary (1997) found that many social workers appeared to lack the time and skills for direct work with children.

Policies, structures and organisation

Within the fostering and research literature, questions have often been asked about the relative merits of different structures in relation to outcomes, but the debate has remained rather inconclusive. From their American study, Stone and Stone (1983) linked success with the way the fostering service was organised in providing post-placement support and training. Rowe *et al* (1984) found many variations in structural arrangements for foster care but could find no clear links between organisational arrangements and outcomes for children. Instead, they placed the emphasis on policies and practices. Nevertheless, they felt that there were many advantages in employing specialist foster care staff and attaching them to area teams rather than centrally. Berridge and Cleaver (1987) identified differences between the authorities they studied with regard to the selection of foster carers, case reviews, and the support offered to carers, but equally concluded that it was essentially differences in practice that produced varying outcomes.

An investigation by the Audit Commission (1994) revealed much variation in the quality of management of fostering schemes and in information available to managers and social workers. Important features

7

of an effective fostering service were identified as:

- regular information on the precise needs of children requiring placements;
- a recruitment process geared to these specific needs;
- an agreement on the aims and outcomes of each placement;
- effective monitoring of outcomes and changing needs;
- adequate support and training for foster carers.

The most recent study on organisational arrangements in England which was undertaken by the NFCA covered 94 out of 107 local authorities responding to a postal questionnaire (Waterhouse, 1997). The researcher identified that in most departments the fostering services had their own distinct team structures within children's services, with their own line management. There was an increasing trend towards complete or partial "purchaser-provider" division arrangements, with the fostering teams located within the provider arm. In 60 per cent of authorities, there was evidence of full or part centralisation of fostering services tasks, especially training and recruitment. Fostering or link workers rarely carried case responsibilities.

Another recent study carried out in Wales revealed that different organisational arrangements existed among the eight authorities depending on geographical and contrasting service philosophies (Pithouse *et al*, 1994). Two of the eight departments were also developing a "purchaser-provider" split. The researchers observed that, whilst policy documents reflected the main themes of the Children Act 1989, they were not "tailored" specifically to foster care. Furthermore, it was asserted that carers and users were not sufficiently involved in policy formulation.

DESIGN, METHODS AND SAMPLING OF THE PRESENT STUDY

The first part of this study focused on foster carers and used a combination of quantitative and qualitative methods. Following consultations with carers and fostering placement staff, separate questionnaires were developed for active and former carers. Both included closed and open-ended questions. Most of the questions asked of the two groups were similar to allow for comparisons. To help provide a check on the material obtained through the questionnaires, group discussions and interviews were also held with around 40 active carers and 27 former ones. Some of the key themes featuring in the postal questionnaire and the interview topics included:

motivation to foster; recruitment, preparation and training; support from social workers and placement or link workers; satisfactions and frustrations; times when they felt like giving up or actually did so and why; the children's parents and contact issues; and views on financial arrangements.

Continuing foster carers

Questionnaires were distributed by the authorities to all the foster carers of seven of the 12 Scottish regional authorities, just before local authority government re-organisation on 1 April 1996. These amounted to a total of 1,132. The sampled authorities were chosen to represent urban, rural and mixed population areas. To complete the picture, we included 52 carers from the only voluntary agency placing an appreciable number of children at the time. (Carers fostering for respite schemes for children with disabilities who were not deemed to be "in care" were excluded from the survey.)

A total of 835 questionnaires (74 per cent) were returned direct to the researchers. We consider this to be a very satisfactory achievement. Thirteen of the questionnaires arrived too late to be included in the analysis which was based on 822 questionnaires. The majority of the questionnaires (53 per cent) were completed jointly by the female and male carers and the rest predominantly by female carers. We have no way of knowing whether the 26 per cent or so of foster carers who failed to respond were very different from those who did but the very good response rate increases the representativeness of the replies. Around nine out of ten respondents chose to give us their home addresses and telephone numbers which made it possible for us to check or ask for more information, when it was felt necessary.

Carers who ceased to foster

The same authorities also provided information on carers who left the service in the two years before the start of the survey. An adapted and shorter questionnaire was sent to them. Data were collected from the following three sources, to ensure greater reliability and accuracy:

i) Questionnaires were sent to former carers from the authorities in the sample who ceased to foster during the two years preceding the start of the study (1994 and 1995). Of 216 former carers identified by the authorities, questionnaires were sent to 201 and 96 (or 48 per cent) responded. At the suggestion of authorities, no questionnaires were sent to 15 former carers because of the circumstances under which they were de-registered by the authority. The response rate was less satisfactory compared to that of active carers.

ii) Information was also gathered from agency records and staff about why the 216 carers stopped. This proved more difficult than originally anticipated, mainly because of incomplete recording and in some cases because of staff changes. In some authorities accurate statistics were kept of who ceased to foster, but not why. Eventually a picture was compiled on 149 (or 69 per cent) of the original 216 who withdrew or were asked to withdraw. Data from this exercise were invaluable in helping to check with the replies received from carers through the postal survey.

iii) Personal non-structured interviews were undertaken with 27 former foster carers who had also completed the questionnaire. These were randomly selected after excluding those who ceased because of retirement. Special emphasis was placed on the reasons for leaving the service and what might have made them stay on or brought them back to fostering.

Policies, organisation and structures

The second part of the study focused on the policies, organisation and structure of all the 32 local authority fostering services in the newly constituted authorities following re-organisation. This also used a combination of quantitative and qualitative methods to obtain information:

i) a postal questionnaire to all 32 authorities;
ii) interviews with managers;

iii) the study of documents;

iv) a census of fostering placements covering the six week period from 15.9.97 to 31.10.97.

i) The questionnaire

Topics were selected following an examination of the research and theoretical literature highlighting themes relevant to the study of policies, structures, organisation and systems for delivering fostering services. In the majority of authorities the questionnaire was completed by a placement service manager and the rest by a senior child care manager. The questionnaire sought information on a range of themes including:

structures and organisational arrangements; fostering policies; recruitment, selection and training of carers; inter-agency collaboration and arrangements with the non-statutory sector; issues of supply and demand; children's social workers and placement workers; the assessment and matching of children; financial issues; panels and reviews; and monitoring and evaluation.

ii) Interviews with managers

Personal interviews with managers aimed to provide a more in-depth understanding of the key issues featured in the questionnaire. The interview was also used to elicit information on policy making and developments which did not feature in the questionnaire.

Half the interviews were with a placement service manager attended also by a senior child care manager (or equivalent). In ten authorities the interview was only with the placement service manager and in another six only with a senior child care manager.

iii) The study of documents

Documents on policy and manuals to staff and foster carers were studied, where available. Many authorities were still using the documents and manuals of the previous regional authorities. The general view expressed by staff was that a lot of thought had gone into the preparation of the previous procedures and only adaptations were needed to bring them up to date with new legislation.

iv) The Census

With the exception of a small and a medium sized authority, all the authorities in Scotland took part in a census which was carried out to establish the demand for different types of placement and how the demand matched with the supply. It covered the six week period between mid-September and the end of October 1997. In discussions with agency staff we were told that this period was as typical as any could be. Authorities were asked to keep the census forms for another two weeks after the end of the census, to include children who had been referred late and might have been found a placement during the extra period.

ANALYSIS AND PRESENTATION OF DATA

The information obtained yielded rich material which was analysed using both quantitative and qualitative methods. Quantitative material was important in allowing us to establish the extent of something taking place or not or the scale of need, whilst qualitative material from the interviews, the questionnaires and the documents was used to illustrate and expand on statistical information. Our overall approach to analysis was based on supportive interaction between quantitative and qualitative data (Brannen, 1992). In this study, reference is mostly made only when a statistically significant relationship had been established. Otherwise, it would have been tedious to repeat each time that no relationship could be found between variables.

STRUCTURE OF THE BOOK

Following this introductory chapter which sets the context of the study, Chapter 2 reports on the structures put in place for the delivery of the fostering services, including systems for quality assurance and quality control, and how the service was organised and managed. Chapter 3 moves on to identify the processes followed for making fostering policy, who influences and who makes policy, the priorities chosen, and emerging policy themes.

Chapter 4 outlines the characteristics and circumstances of current foster carers and how similar or different they are from the general population. It covers age, status, own children, and carers' ages and life styles. The next chapter looks at recruitment from the perspective of carers and authorities. It covers what brought carers into fostering, the recruitment methods that influenced them most, and the recruitment processes and methods used by authorities. Chapter 6 examines the authorities' response to inquiries, and the methods used for the assessment, preparation and training of foster carers.

The issue of supply and demand of foster carers and the results of the six week fostering referral survey are reported in Chapter 7. Chapter 8 identifies the types of fostering undertaken and the kinds of children fostered. It also records the best and worst aspects of fostering as seen by carers and whether their expectations in relation to fostering were met or not.

How the carers' own children experience fostering is dealt with in Chapter 9. This is followed by a chapter on the issue of contact between children and their families. Chapter 11 reports on the delivery of the fostering services as perceived by carers and managers and examines the role of the child's social worker and that of the placement worker. Chapter 12 continues by reporting on the assessment of children and the matching process followed within authorities. It identifies impediments to matching, including carer shortages, and goes on to discuss the participation of children, their parents and carers in selecting placements and drawing up agreements.

The concept of support and its components are set out in Chapter 13. Chapter 14 goes on to report on carers who cease to foster and why. The views of carers on the financial arrangements and the schemes set up by the authorities for the payment of carers are discussed in Chapter 15. Finally, the concluding chapter brings together and debates the major themes that arose from both parts of the study and makes recommendations for possible action.

Notes
In all the tables and figures, percentages in most cases have been rounded up to the nearest point.

2 Organisation and management

This chapter examines the overall organisational and management structures adopted by local authorities for the delivery of their fostering services. Within the fostering and research literature, questions have often been asked about the relative merits of different organisational structures in relation to foster care outcomes. There has been reference to structures influencing the selection of foster carers, case reviews, the support offered to carers (Stone and Stone, 1983; Berridge and Cleaver, 1987) and outcomes for children (Rowe *et al*, 1989) but the debate has remained inconclusive. Until the recent studies by Pithouse *et al* (1994) in Wales, Waterhouse (1997) and partly Rowe *et al* (1989) in England, no other research has tried to identify in detail the organisational structures set up by local authorities UK wide for the delivery and monitoring of fostering services.

THE LOCAL AUTHORITY STRUCTURES

The great majority of local authorities in Scotland in 1996 had set up separate social work departments (26 or 81 per cent) headed by a director of social work and answerable to a council social work committee. A minority (six) had combined social work with housing and, at the time of writing, two other authorities were contemplating doing the same. None of the English authorities had gone down that route when data were collected in 1995 (Waterhouse, 1997).

Whilst the majority of authorities in Scotland described traditional hierarchical overall management structures, others had adopted so called "corporate" systems aiming for more flexible boundaries between different service sectors. This was claimed to suit particularly small authorities and to lead to a more economical use of resources. For example, in one authority, a development manager combined planning, housing and social work. A health services manager managed all domicilliary care services. In another authority all children's services were considered under a single Children's Committee, covering the education of children,

children looked after and the youth services. Similar to the overall "corporate" structures were the so called "flat" systems adopted by a number of social work departments which also aimed for flexible boundaries between service sections and between higher management and front line staff. It again resulted in a smaller number of top managers carrying several portfolios, rather than specialising in a single area identified either with service provision or a client group.

It was claimed that, in authorities with "corporate" type structures and within social work departments with "flat" type systems, the interests of the fostering service could be promoted or held back, depending on the background of this person and their interest in social work, child care or foster care.

THE ORGANISATION AND MANAGEMENT OF THE FOSTERING SERVICE

In nine out of ten authorities in Scotland, a clear functional separation was observed between children's and adult services at planning and resource provider level. Mainly because of geographical and demo-graphic considerations, no such separation existed in the remaining authorities. A broadly similar picture was found in England (Waterhouse, 1997). Irrespective of how the new authorities had organised themselves, fostering had a distinctive place within the children and family services of all authorities. However, three authorities in Scotland had split the foster care of adolescents from other forms of fostering and passed responsibility for this age group onto their youth services section under criminal justice. Conversely, several others who had this arrangement in the past had subsequently brought together all types of fostering.

In almost four out of five Scottish authorities (82 per cent), the fostering service was split in two parts. With the exception of three county councils, this was also true of 97 per cent of English authorities (Waterhouse, 1997). The two parts of the fostering service were meant to work closely together, even though they were often physically separated. One part came under the umbrella term of "family placement" (or equivalent) and the other under fieldwork child care services. The family placement part of the service mainly covered the recruitment, selection and support aspects of fostering, adoption, respite care, supported lodgings and day care. More exceptionally it also covered throughcare, residential care and after care. Depending on the agency, the family placement service might operate from central or district units or be based in area teams (see later).

The fieldwork branch of the fostering service was operated by social workers based within area child care teams. Besides other child care responsibilities, such as child protection, these workers carried responsibility for the child or young person in foster care.

The size of an authority or the number of carers managed by each one was not always a guide to the way the fostering service would be organised. Big and small authorities adopted both similar and different organisational structures. Our interviews suggest that structures, beliefs, demography, geography and tradition all played some part in dictating the organisational structure of the fostering services. Each adopted model was strongly defended. Carers were reported not to have had much say in the organisational and managerial structures adopted by the new councils.

The management of the fostering service
In most authorities there was a single top manager responsible for the management of the child and family services. Further down, the line management split into different sections including, in most authorities, separate managers for the delivery of the fostering service, that is, services to foster carers and services to the child and his/her family. In seven out of ten of the Scottish authorities, placement workers and children's social workers had separate line management structures. In England this was true of almost all authorities (Waterhouse, 1997).

In authorities with placement service managers, the placement and area child care teams operated largely independently of each other, except that they both came under the head of child care services or equivalent at the middle and higher levels of management (see later in this chapter). This arrangement had the advantage of giving the place-ment service direct access to higher management, but required good co-ordination to ensure an integrated approach between the placement service and area child care team managers and staff. Where good co-ordination was not achieved, it gave rise to tensions between these two sections of the service, which are discussed at greater length later in the book.

In two-fifths of Scottish authorities no placement service manager's post existed. Line management responsibilities, in this case, were carried by the head of child care, or the area team manager, or an operational manager operating below the head of child care. In three big authorities the placement service was based in districts, each of which had in place a placement organiser, but again there was no overall placement manager to represent the whole fostering service. Placement staff in authorities with no placement manager in post felt that the omission deprived them of leadership and contributed to the marginalisation of the service.

Change and stability in the fostering service

Only around two-fifths of Scottish and just under half of English authorities reported that their fostering service had reached organisational stability (see Table 2:1). The remainder either said that it was currently changing or that it was subject to review and possibly changes in the future. The continuing changes and reviews were partly a reverberation from the recent local government re-organisation. Other factors were resource restraints; moving from area based to centrally based fostering staff and vice versa; and new ways of looking at service delivery e.g. in some agencies the relationship between the residential and fostering services. Lack of service stability is bound to impact on the quality of service delivery.

Table 2.1

Extent of organisational stability of the fostering service

	Scotland %	England* %
Stable	37	47
Changing	25	29
Review/possible change	37	24
Total	99	100

Source: Waterhouse, 1997.

Models of organisation and the location of the service

Three-quarters of Scottish authorities maintained a clear delineation between placement workers whose main duties were to address the servicing of foster homes and social workers whose duties involved case responsibility for children and their families. This also meant that almost all foster carers had a placement worker allocated to them. Where a clear delineation occurred, placement workers carried no child care case loads. In most of the remaining authorities, a partial delineation prevailed, with some staff within the same agency doing so and others not. Overall, only less than half of English authorities appeared to allocate all approved carers to a named placement worker (Waterhouse, 1997). Much more in England than in Scotland, long-term carers and kinship carers had no specialist help and all support was left up to the area team social worker.

This study identified the following three main models around which the delivery of placement services was organised in Scotland.

i)   Centrally/divisionally based placement units (65% of authorities)
ii)   Area team attachments (16% of authorities)
iii)   Generic and mixed child care teams (18% of authorities)

i) Centrally/divisionally based placement units

The predominant model of organisation adopted by two in three authorities in Scotland, for the delivery of placement services, was of a unit operating from a single point at the centre or from a divisional district office. Centralised units and placement staff were not only organisationally separate from area teams, but in many authorities they were also physically separate from them. The unit staff were expected to provide the area teams with fostering placements, to act as support workers to carers and also carry out all the other functions associated with the placement worker's role. In these authorities case responsibility and services to the child and the child's family were carried by social workers specialising in child care and based in area teams (see Figure 2.1).

Figure 2.1
Centralised model

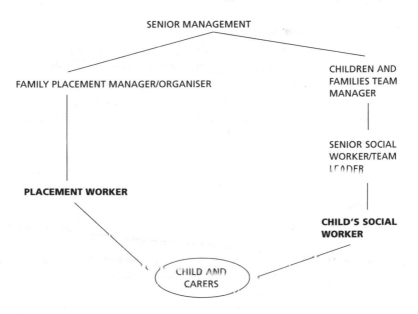

ii) Area team based placement staff

The second model to emerge was of specialist placement workers being attached to area teams from where they carried out their family placement and other fostering responsibilities. This model was adopted by five (16 per cent) of the authorities. Within this model, family placement staff carried no case responsibilities either for foster children or for any other child care work. Case responsibility was undertaken by children's social workers in the same team who were also carrying child protection and family work caseloads.

As with units, these staff were usually, but not always, managed by a resource/service family placement manager who was either centrally or divisionally based. More exceptionally they were managed by area team seniors or area Children and Families managers. Some family placement staff found this last arrangement unsatisfactory on the ground that their

19

first line managers were unfamiliar with family placement work, including the literature and research on the subject.

iii) Area based generic/mixed

A variant to the above model was one recently introduced by four authorities, but also used already by two others, where all Children and Families staff were based in area teams. Besides undertaking work with a child in foster care, they also acted as link workers to carers. However, the same worker was not usually supposed to be both link worker and child's social worker for the same fostering household, though it was not unknown. In many respects the separation of the two roles continued, except that the staff came from a basically "generic" child care team.

Which model?

Arguments for and against centrally or area team based placement staff were well articulated by both sides and are set out in Table 2.2. A powerful argument put forward by some unit managers in defence of units was that these were easily identifiable and accessible to foster carers with whom they had established high levels of contact and rapport:

Carers can easily identify with the unit as a family placement service with staff committed to it. There are identifiable seniors and an identifiable manager. If they ring up and they can't get one person they are as happy to talk to another because they know them.

The above argument was put in the context of the difficulties many carers were experiencing in getting in touch with staff in area teams, often leading to frustration and disillusionment. When placement staff, it was argued, are attached to area teams, fostering work is seen by others in the team as being an "extra" to the core of their work and their fostering time is eroded as a result. The loss of technical expertise, isolation from colleagues and missing out on new developments were other quoted disadvantages. One manager described the loss as follows:

There is a loss around the technical ends and the development of the fostering staff. The individual workers pay a price because they are dispersed.

The main advantages claimed for the attachment model were closer communication and co-operation between children's social workers and placement workers and fewer tensions between the two parts of the service.

Whether family placement staff were based centrally, divisionally or in area teams, they were meant to co-operate closely and share placements across the whole agency. In practice, problems were evident when it came to the sharing of placements between teams.

Table 2.1

Advantages claimed for unit based and area team based placement staff

Advantages claimed on behalf of central units	Advantages claimed on behalf of area team attachments
• a uniform and consistent service	• better co-ordination with area team and CSW*
• protection of placement workers' time from area team pressures	• fewer tensions between placement staff and CSWs
• overall view of placement resources for better matching	• more attuned to the needs of area teams
• keeping up-to-date with specialist knowledge, expertise and research	• less inward looking compared to units
• contributing to changes from an informed position	• speedy information gathering and sharing leading to better assessment and matching
• easier to cover for absent staff and respond to carers' concerns	• diffuses "unhealthy" over -identification with foster carers

CSW = Child's Social Worker

THE LOCATION OF KEY FOSTERING SERVICES

The most centralised activity was the approval of carers by panels (77 per cent), followed by the review of carers (71 per cent) and then recruitment campaigns and training. By contrast the assessment of carers was as likely to be decentralised as centralised. There were no significant differences between Scotland and England on the extent of decentralisa-tion except that the assessment of carers was more likely to be decentral-ised in Scotland than in England.

Connections between fostering and other local authority family placement services

Out of the 32 Scottish authorities answering the question, 26 indicated that they operated a placement fostering service which was linked to other related services such as adoption, respite care and sometimes day care and throughcare. Furthermore, in 58 per cent of the authorities, compared to 71 per cent in England, fostering and adoption were organised under the same structure. In another five authorities, fostering was part of a wider service for children and families and in a further six it was a mixture of these two approaches.

Birth records counselling, adoption work and supported lodgings for looked after children were services managed or partly managed and provided as part of the fostering service structure but not subject to the fostering regulations. Private fostering could be managed either by the placement service or area teams.

LINKS BETWEEN FOSTERING AND RESIDENTIAL SERVICES

Fostering and residential care are the main forms of provision used for accommodating children looked after away from home. It was also noted earlier that a handful of authorities were moving towards the greater integration of their fostering placement and residential services. The close relationship and inter-dependence between these two forms of care have always been recognised, especially the knowledge that some older children move between the two (Rowe *et al*, 1989; Triseliotis *et al*, 1995a; Sinclair *et al*, 1995).

The managerial arrangements

At the higher levels of management and planning, the majority of Scottish authorities (72 per cent), compared with 61 per cent in England, had a shared management structure for their family placement and residential services for children. Five others had separate management arms and the remaining four either had other arrangements or were still to decide.

In only a fifth of authorities did shared management continue down to middle and first line management levels. Almost a third of Scottish authorities and a similar proportion in England allowed for flexibility of budgets between fostering and residential services. On the whole, smaller authorities in Scotland went for greater budget flexibility compared to the bigger ones.

STANDBY PROVISION

Many authorities in Scotland were still operating and sharing general standby services (or a round-the-clock emergency service), as set up by the former regional authorities, and there were indications that this arrangement would continue. It was the carers' view that standby staff, whilst trying to be helpful, were not very successful because they often lacked the understanding and expertise that went with fostering. At such times most authorities expected carers, especially new ones, to seek the informal support of more experienced carers. However, as many carers told the study, whilst peers and family can prove very supportive, there are also times when carers want and need to share a concern with someone carrying authority and formal responsibility.

SPECIAL SCHEMES

Special arrangements for adolescents
Almost half the Scottish authorities, about the same as in England, had specialist schemes, and in some cases separate specialist teams, for adolescents. In three authorities the schemes were attached to the youth sections of criminal justice focusing on this age group. Another two authorities had delegated responsibility for the foster care of adolescents to a voluntary agency. Separate schemes largely operated as a service within a service, with different financial rewards for carers and some-times separate recruitment campaigns and separate selection procedures.

Several small authorities which did not have such a scheme were hoping to start one, whilst a couple of those who had schemes were planning to integrate them with the rest of fostering. It was argued that, besides rivalries among carers, the original assumption that carers would find adolescents more difficult to manage than younger children was no longer sustainable. Most children, it was argued, presented challenging problems. We will see in a later chapter that these views were substantiated by the carers' perception of the children's difficulties.

Special arrangements for children with disabilities

Almost nine out of ten Scottish authorities had special respite care schemes for looked after children with disabilities. Just under half of English authorities had separate schemes but possibly more made such a resource available, but not under a specialist scheme (Waterhouse, 1997). Three small Scottish authorities were offering the schemes jointly. Another two commissioned a voluntary agency to provide the service and two others were considering doing the same. All the schemes were run by the family placement service except in two authorities where responsibility was delegated to their respective area teams.

PURCHASER/PROVIDER SPLITS

In this context we mean by purchaser/provider split the allocation of budgets to area teams for the purchase of fostering services either from the independent/voluntary sector or from their agency's placement service. One agency had a fully operational scheme, four others had a partly operational one and two others had plans to introduce one. Two thirds of the Scottish authorities were not operating and had no plans to operate a purchaser/provider split within their children's services. In England, 45 per cent of authorities reported that they had created purchaser/provider splits for their services, although only slightly more than half had set up separate cost centres and independent accounting systems (Waterhouse, 1997, p 17). Only two out of the eight Welsh authorities were using the split (Pithouse et al, 1994).

Advantages claimed on behalf of fully or partially operating purchaser/provider schemes in Scotland included: clearer aims; being needs led; ring-fenced time to develop "good quality" resources; greater flexibility and easier monitoring.

The main disadvantage identified was that the system was giving rise to tensions between purchaser and provider sectors within the agency, and also between authorities, because of the way services were beginning to be costed, sometimes without consultation. There was an emerging feeling, too, that the children's "best interests" were being obscured or sidelined in the pursuit of either cheaper services or of accounting efficiency.

Berridge (1997) quotes a publication by Jones and Bilton (1994) who concluded that purchaser/provider separation is not an appropriate model for the organisation of children's services (p 54). They assert that daily care providers often have the best insight into children's needs and artificial separation from care managers is likely to be unhelpful. Berridge adds that greater fragmentation of roles may also endanger effective communication between professionals, which could have important consequences for child protection. A more recent study concluded that the purchaser/provider splits had not only lower fostering percentages, compared to those of the functional departments, but that costs were 50 per cent higher. The article went on to add that 'costs in an externalised resource will tend to move towards market costs, in this case upwards' (Richards, 1999, p 28).

VOLUNTARY, INDEPENDENT AND OTHER PLACEMENT ARRANGEMENTS

Two-thirds of the Scottish authorities were using placements provided by voluntary agencies but only two authorities used placements from the independent sector. This form of contracting out an aspect of the fostering service was usually done on an individual basis, that is, as spot purchasing rather than on a block allocation. Though the English figures do not separate voluntary from independent placements, they show that 73 per cent of authorities were using both types of placements.

In all, only 67 of all the fostering placement units being used by local authorities in Scotland at the time of the survey were externally provided. The highest number of units used by a single authority was 15 (or 13 per cent of its "in-house" stock) and the lowest was one. Most authorities used two to three units. Authorities with purchaser/provider schemes were no more or less likely to use external placements than others. Local authorities in England used a much higher proportion of placements provided by other sectors. For example, one inner London borough's use of approved carers from other sectors represented 31 per cent of its carers (Waterhouse, 1997).

JOINT ARRANGEMENTS BETWEEN AUTHORITIES

A number of areas of work suggested themselves for possible collaboration between clusters of the 32 Scottish new unitary authorities, but primary consideration was given to inter-agency placements. The majority of authorities had joint arrangements for this, including two-fifths for support to carers and three authorities which had arrangements for the joint approval of foster carers. The arrangements for joint placements were a carry-over from the previous authorities. As one example, a number of authorities which were formerly part of Strathclyde continued to operate a centrally based emergency placement system.

Authorities were currently setting up working groups and holding discussions amongst themselves with a view to finding ways for sharing certain activities and resources, such as for recruitment, training and placements or the sharing of standby services, without necessarily operating a distinct market. Most attention was being paid to the "exchange" or "borrowing" of placements but the costing of such placements presented serious problems between "lenders" and "receivers".

ASSURING AND CONTROLLING QUALITY

Table 2.3 brings together the kind of systems put in place by Scottish and English authorities which were seen as exercising a kind of quality assurance and quality control role and which could be used for the evaluation also of the service. Many of the measures put in place largely reflected legal obligations. Though the systems and mechanisms outlined below were said to be in place, they were not consistently observed or applied because of staff shortages.

Table 2.3

Proportion of authorities having in place quality assurance and quality control systems

		Scotland %	England* %
i)	Written statements regarding quality standards required in foster homes	66	56
ii)	Manual for carers	87	64
iii)	Fostering panel in place	100	97
iv	Recording annual rate of breakdowns	28	20
v)	Reviews carried out within specified times	66	39
vi)	Systematic feedback from carers	59	18
vii)	Written allegation procedures	78	Not available
viii)	Overall foster carer involvement	27	34

*Source: Waterhouse, 1997.

Only around one in five authorities in both Scotland and England said they had systems that allowed them to monitor and collate information on the recruitment and loss of carers, placement disruptions and placement outcomes, the ethnicity of carers and the profile of children requiring placement. As with general monitoring systems, no systematic standards and success measures for carers were found in place, though several authorities were developing them and others said they were waiting for the expected publication of National Standards.

USE OF MANAGEMENT INFORMATION SYSTEMS

The majority of authorities in both Scotland and England had not yet installed sophisticated information technology systems for use as tools to aid practitioners, managers and policy makers. For example, Table 2.4 shows that less than a fifth of authorities had in place information systems that would enable them to monitor a wide range of policy and practice issues and help them, especially, to make connections between supply and demand of placements and in the matching of children. A number of authorities were hoping to move in that direction, but some were pessimistic about how possible it would be to develop them and keep them up-to-date at a time of serious budgetary constraints.

Table 2.4
Proportion of authorities using management information systems

	Scotland %	England* %*
Record basic information about carers	47	90
Access foster home vacancies by computer	25	31
Match carer and child	9	14
Monitor recruitment	19	22
Monitor loss of carers	22	22
Monitor outcome of placements	16	20
Monitor disruption rates	16	20
Monitor ethnicity of carers	19	40
Monitor the profile of children requiring placement	16	12

Source: Waterhouse, 1997.

SUMMARY

- Considerable uniformity was found in the way the fostering service was organised, managed and delivered.
- In the majority of authorities in both England and Scotland, the structure and organisation of the service was said to be changing or under review leading to a sense of instability.
- In nine out of ten Scottish authorities and almost all the English ones, a clear functional division was observed between children and families services and adult services at fieldwork and resource provider level.
- In 82 per cent of authorities in Scotland and 96 per cent of surveyed authorities in England, family placement workers and fieldworkers had a separate management structure.
- Three-quarters of the Scottish authorities maintained a clear delineation between foster carer support undertaken by placement workers and case responsibility undertaken by children's social workers.
- A variety of organisational models for the fostering placement service was found in Scotland, but the predominant one (65 per cent) was of centrally or divisionally based units. Area team attachments and/or fully decentralised placement staff also existed.

- Most fostering service tasks (recruitment, assessment, approval of carers, training and carer review) were fully or part centralised.
- In around seven out of ten authorities in both England and Scotland, foster and residential care had shared management structures at the higher levels but only in a small number of authorities did this continue to lower line management levels.
- It was very common for authorities in Scotland to have respite schemes for children with disabilities and almost half had special schemes for adolescents. Less than half of authorities in England reported having specialist teams or schemes operating within the fostering service.
- One third of authorities in Scotland and just under half in England were said to be operating some kind of purchaser/provider scheme.
- In contrast to England, an insignificant proportion of children were fostered by the non-statutory sector in Scotland, possibly because of the high cost.
- The relative absence of management information systems was hampering the monitoring and evaluation of the fostering service.

3 The making of fostering policy

INTRODUCTION

This chapter examines the processes followed for the making of fostering policy within the 32 Scottish local authorities, including who initiates and makes fostering policy and the priorities chosen. In addition, the chapter examines how fostering policy was responding to the short-comings of the service identified by carers and managers. (To the best of our knowledge, no study has focused on fostering policy making in England.)

WRITTEN FOSTERING POLICY

Acknowledging that the term "policy" is an ambiguous and controversial one, it was not always easy to identify whether specific fostering policy existed and if so where. With several notable exceptions, there was a general lack of tradition for setting out detailed aims and objectives of fostering policies in writing or of setting out longer term strategies. This was attributed by many managers to the low profile of fostering within many authorities which also adversely affected the attraction of re-sources. Pithouse *et al* (1994) too reported that policy documents of the Welsh authorities reflected the general child care themes of the Children Act 1989, but they were not "tailored" specifically to foster care.

Written statements about child and family services did not often include specific aims and objectives on fostering policy in such areas as resourcing, recruitment, training, the provision of different types of fostering services, support services, partnership, the needs of children with disabilities and those of minority ethnic groups. Some managers argued that this was a transitory period and that clearer fostering policies with more specific aims and objectives on a number of activities would not emerge until after their Children's Services Plans were finalised. Others pointed out that specific policies were to be found in the guidance, procedures and manuals which were waiting to be updated.

We were told that within the new unitary councils many councillors and some senior managers were new to children's services and fostering and that perhaps more time was needed to raise the fostering service's image, profile and needs. In the meantime, a number of managers felt frustrated that the service was run on short-term objectives with the longer term perspective missing: 'no explicit strategy', 'nothing in writing in any detail' or 'no vision, no strategy'.

Existing fostering policy rarely went beyond generalities. The most common aim stated was 'for community type responses' and/or that:

All children should have access to family life with resources being channelled towards keeping them in their own homes and in the community.

However, several authorities which had finalised their children's services plans did provide somewhat more detail on their fostering policies. Besides general value statements, they also spelled out some specific objectives concerning services to children, young people and their families including: the resolve to train and support carers; accept a long-term commitment on behalf of children who had been looked after by the authority; work in partnership with parents, carers and users and involve them in policy development; and also take account of a child's religious, linguistic, racial and cultural background. For example, within the Children's and Family Plans of one authority, there was the general commitment:

to develop a range of services and resources, work in partnership with carers, parents and the community in order to keep the children in the community.

Another authority went somewhat further by declaring its resolve for family based care resources, including:

a range of skilled and well supported carers who can meet the assessed needs of children who require to be looked after and placed.

Considering, however, that fostering is now the major form of substitute care provided to children looked after away from home, it did not feature in any major way within most authorities' emerging strategic planning.

INITIATING AND PROMOTING FOSTERING POLICY

The specialist nature of family placement work meant that service and resource managers were the most likely ones to initiate and promote fostering policy changes in consultation with team leaders, fostering staff and senior child care management. Not surprisingly, their views were usually sought by planning and working groups set up to review child care policies. If it were not for this group of specialist staff exercising continued pressure and lobbying, fostering policy would not, apparently, have been given much priority. Foster carers too put their trust in placement staff to take things up on their behalf and on behalf of the children:

> If it wasn't for them link workers, others would not have bothered much.

Where the post of placement service manager did not exist, the responsibility to promote fostering policy was more diffuse. It fell mainly on the head of child care services (or equivalent) to do so, and that person might not have the time or remit to promote foster care.

Mechanisms for collating information
In order to respond to the new legal requirements, and to update their own policies, procedures and practices, authorities had set up committees and/or planning groups to collate information and put forward proposals to councils for their Children's Services Plans. In the majority of authorities, deliberations were still in process at the time of the visits. Three such mechanisms were identified by the study, the first two were formal and the third informal and ad hoc.

i) Children's Services Planning Committees
Mainly to fulfil their new legal obligations, the majority of authorities set up some kind of Children's Services Planning Committee to collect evidence, mainly from working groups, and make proposals for possible adaptations to existing child care policies and plans, including foster care. It was still too early to say how successful working groups would be in persuading Children's Services Planning Committees to recognise

and prioritise the interests of the fostering service, beyond what was legally required. Reactions to them, so far, were mixed ranging from enthusiasm at one end to scepticism and some despair at the other. Much, we were told, depended on who represented the interests of the fostering service at the decision making stage, especially in authorities with "corporate" or "flat" management structures.

ii) Multi-agency strategy groups

In a minority of authorities all policy issues, including fostering, were considered by what were called "multi-agency strategy" groups or corporate planning groups or their equivalent. These were usually composed of senior managers from all services such as housing, education, social work, the police, health and sometimes the voluntary sector. They were mostly chaired by the council's Chief Executive. Like review committees, multi-agency strategy groups would also set up working parties to report to them on specific sectors of service such as children and families.

Though the general idea of multi-agency and functional committees for policy making was positively regarded, there were also a number of reservations. In the first place, procedures for collecting evidence were not always well defined. It was also felt that fostering issues were being lost within such broadly based structures where education and housing, along with child protection, appeared to dominate thinking. Such committees were generally seen as far removed from the daily concerns of the fostering service, the pressures it was facing, and its priorities.

iii) Individual efforts and initiatives

In a small number of authorities (19 per cent) where no formal review or planning child care committees had yet been set up, fostering policy was apparently largely left to individual initiatives by default. Individuals could be heads of child care, a senior family placement service manager or a placement team leader. Any of these managers might take the initiative to produce proposals for an aspect of fostering policy but only for absolutely minimum adaptations or changes mainly to meet new legal requirements.

This ad hoc arrangement came more often, but not exclusively, from authorities where social work was combined with other services, such as housing. The process was generally perceived as highly unsatisfactory, as too ad hoc, and as lacking in purpose and direction. Placement managers in these authorities felt marginalised:

no policy development, no debate yet, no formal mechanisms.

Resourcing and prioritising needs

The making of policy and the resourcing of the fostering service are two closely connected activities. The prevailing view in most authorities was that the resource capacity of the new decentralised authorities was limited for some of their child care functions. Councils, we were told, were anxious to contain spending within existing budgets and even make cuts to meet government spending limits. As a result, meeting future foster care standards without additional resourcing is likely to prove problematic, especially for the smaller councils.

In answer to the question of whether any of the recent changes or contemplated ones related to budgetary restraints, of the 27 authorities answering this question 15 (or 55 per cent) said 'no', six (or 22 per cent) said 'yes' and the remainder conveyed a mixed picture. In discussions, service managers indicated that the main constraints operating on the fostering service were not so much in maintaining the existing levels of provision, but in developing the service in ways that took account of its shortcomings, of the carers' rising aspirations and of market realities. As an example, in some authorities vacancies for child care posts were kept vacant because of the 'severe' financial constraints faced by them and staff were expected to offer cover 'as if nothing had happened'. In a couple of authorities many children's cases were said to have remained unallocated. A typical message coming from councillors and/or top managers was:

Update policies and procedures to reflect the new Act, but without involving increased expenditure. Council priorities are mainly in housing, education and child protection.

Any resources needed for new developments had to come from restructuring and even then it was not certain whether money saved, for example, from closing residential units, would go towards the development of the fostering service. Child protection, narrowly defined, seemed to dominate child care policy and practice in ways that relegated crucial other work with looked after children, such as those in foster care, to secondary importance.

Resources and status become attached to child protection and other services suffer.

The setting of priorities in most authorities was inevitably influenced by the prevailing climate of serious resource limitations. As a result, greater priority was given to meeting the requirements of the new Act, than on new developments such as recruitment, more direct support to children and carers, and the carers' conditions of service.

On the whole, considerable interest and momentum were found to promote new initiatives and new fostering policies. In authorities where senior and top management, along with councillors, took a personal interest in fostering and in foster carers, limited and sometimes longer term developments were also spearheaded. Typical comments of the advantages of having sympathetic top management and councillors included:

They have a strong political commitment to foster care, including the commitment of resources.

In contrast, in a few authorities, a number of councillors, top managers and even some front line staff were said to be still looking upon foster caring as a largely charitable activity. As a consequence, committees, far from examining ways to develop the service or respond to the aspirations of carers, were even looking for cuts:

Councillors view fostering as being done out of the "goodness" of the carer's heart.

Or

Top and senior managers know little about social work or fostering. They have no idea what kind of children are placed and what carers are expected to do.

THE CONTRIBUTION OF STAKEHOLDERS TO FOSTERING POLICY

Children, young people and parents

There were no formal systems in place for the representation on committees or working groups of young people who were or had recently been in foster care. Great reliance was placed on social workers to consult with them and their parents and convey their views to the working groups. In some authorities, more formal methods of consultation were mainly meant to be through Who Cares? Trust and Children's Rights Officers employed by a number of authorities. We were told, however, that in many of these authorities the system was either under review or in abeyance.

The contribution of carers

No examples were found of carers routinely being invited to sit as members of Children's Services Planning Committees. However, a fifth of authorities said that they regularly invited carers to sit on working groups making suggestions to review and planning committees, whilst most of the rest said 'sometimes' and several 'never'. Some added that input by carers was 'informal' or 'unusual'. Other comments were:

Very difficult for carers to influence policy except through reviews.
Or
Carers' input is through reviews, groups and link workers.

Most consultation with carers remained mainly at the informal level between placement workers and family placement staff and carers. A more formal example was that of several authorities successfully running consultation groups with their carers which met from four to six times a year. A handful of others were trying hard to revive similar forums run by the previous authorities. Examples were also quoted of carers not being interested to contribute to policy making, or not having the time, or both. The few carers who commented on this referred to the many other demands made on their time with no additional remuneration. Some contrasted this with staff who were paid for all their time, including when sitting on committees and working groups.

Although carers identified a number of strengths in the fostering service, they also reported a number of serious shortcomings. Service and senior managers were not totally unaware of some of these. However, at the time of the interviews, there was no evidence that the key concerns expressed by carers were being addressed. We outline two of the main concerns below.

i) Support to children and foster carers

The most frequent criticisms offered by carers were about lack of support to children in foster care and their carers by social workers. These mainly had to do with infrequent visits, unavailability, unresponsiveness, lack of information on the children, lack of team work and lack of consultation. Most of these deficiencies were attributed to resource and organisational problems, but occasionally unhelpful professional or personal attitudes were highlighted. (This topic is explored further in subsequent chapters.)

ii) Payment for carers and conditions of service

No new policies were emerging to provide for improved payments to carers and improvements to their conditions of service. Little account seemed to be taken yet of the different climate and economic conditions within which fostering was now beginning to operate and of the aspirations of carers. All evidence suggests that this process is likely to accelerate over the coming years.

Consultations with other services

Foster care is not solely a social work provision. It interacts with other services mainly education, health, housing and the judiciary. The success of a placement may be as much related to these as to social work activities. Social workers should be able to tap into these services and strategic planning in an authority would need to provide for this.

In some authorities, the requirement to produce Children's Services Plans was used as a springboard to bring together other council services, outside authorities, and the voluntary sector to look at policy developments affecting children. Discussions with education services were usually in the context of developing youth strategies and some notable collaborative achievements were described. Examples were also quoted where such consultations and collaboration were proving constructive and helpful in raising awareness about child care need and in raising the profile of foster care. Collaborative arrangements at the general policy level should ideally set the pattern and create the climate for close collaboration in individual cases such as the schooling of a child or the provision of specialist health services (e.g. psychiatric).

Closer interaction between social work and housing resulted in a number of authorities providing bigger houses, or making alterations to existing ones, for approved carers who needed more space. We found no authority, though, willing to do so for prospective carers. Since then the House of Commons Health Committee Report (1998, p 36) has urged for co-operation between social services and housing departments to ensure that potential foster carers were not deterred from taking on this role by that lack of suitable accommodation.

PLACEMENTS WITH RELATIVES

The number of approved relative foster carers in 1997 in Scotland was around one in ten, broadly similar to that found in England (Waterhouse, 1997). Policies on placements with relatives varied widely between authorities. Besides Rowe *et al*'s (1984) study, no other recent study has examined in detail the precise strengths and limitations of relative placements, but such placements were posing a number of concerns to managers and practitioners. They included many relatives' limited resources, their inability, sometimes, to protect children from abuse from within the family, the criminal records of some of them, and often their reluctance to work with social workers. Nevertheless, there was awareness that with family conferences being on the increase, family placements were also likely to increase.

Some authorities were considerably exercised about how to treat those fostering related children and they were finding it difficult to decide exactly what status to ascribe to them. A minority felt that the Guidance to the Children (Scotland) Act 1995 fudged the issue almost as much as the policies of previous regional authorities. With some exceptions, there was a general reluctance in the recent past to consider children placed with relatives as being formally fostered. As a result, few former regional authorities had explicit written policies on the matter and the same approach continued under the new authorities. Policy was largely improvised to suit local circumstances.

The previous preference for "informality" and "improvisation" was followed for two main reasons: first, it was thought inappropriate to stigmatise the children by "sucking" them into the care system. Second, it was thought by some authorities that paying relatives allowances or fees would generate envy and possibly conflict between the child's parents and the relatives undertaking the caring. Because of this, the great majority paid these carers less than the normal fostering allowances out of section 12 money (Social Work (Scotland) Act, 1968). The allowance could be a third or a half of the normal weekly allowance. The lower allowance took account of the fact that relatives on benefits or income support would also be able to top it up with benefits and claim child benefit as well.

Further reasons for not wanting to treat relatives as formal carers appeared to be the additional expenditure involved and the amount of time it would take staff to carry out full home studies and provide the usual pre and post-placement support services or allocate them a link worker. There was also the knowledge that some relatives would not meet the assessment criteria for becoming foster carers, yet it would be in the interests of the children to be placed with them because of existing bonds. Almost all such placements were the responsibility of hard pressed area teams rather than the placement service.

THE MONITORING OF THE FOSTERING SERVICE

The fostering service often lacked standards and performance criteria of systematic monitoring and management information systems to establish what was happening on the ground and the changes and adaptations which might be necessary at the policy, management or practice levels. For assuring and controlling the quality of their fostering services, most authorities relied on having in place the statutory required panels and review committees, and on senior management to monitor developments.

SUMMARY

- The profile of fostering within many local authorities was said to be low, adversely affecting policy development and resourcing.
- Fostering policy was generally submerged within general child care policy. Specific details on fostering policy accompanied by strategic planning were difficult to find.
- Serious resource limitations appeared to be hampering the development of the service to enable it to respond to new needs and circumstances. As a result, the emerging policies were not addressing some key limitations of the service identified by carers and staff.
- A significant number of service managers felt marginalised and were not hopeful of achieving much change.
- The contribution of carers, young people and parents to fostering policy formulation, planning and decision-making was mainly unsystematic.

4 Who are the foster carers?

This chapter describes the main personal and social characteristics of carers in Scotland, their household composition and life styles. There has been no recent comprehensive study in England, but reference is made to any comparable information available.

BACKGROUND CHARACTERISTICS

Knowledge of the characteristics of carers can indicate how far they are similar or different from others in the community. Knowing the characteristics of carers who continue to foster and of those who cease, can also help recruitment by identifying which specific groups should be targeted. There is a further value, in that certain characteristics, such as age or the number and ages of own children, have been found by some studies to contribute to the greater stability or breakdown of placements.

Age of carers

When they started fostering, most carers were then aged 31–40 (Table 4.1). Overall, three out of five female carers and 53 per cent of males were 40 and under at the time. At the time of the survey, however, around seven in ten female and eight in ten male carers were now over the age of 40. Almost half the single carers in this survey were over the age of 50 at the time of the survey. Some studies have associated the older age of foster carers with better outcomes (Parker, 1966; Triseliotis, 1980). The shift in age groups from younger carers at the start to older ones at the time of the survey suggests a fair amount of continuity of carers but these proportions also highlight the under-representation of both female and male new carers in their 40s and early 50s.

Table 4.1
Age of female/male carers in Scotland when they started fostering and now

	Female carer		Male carer	
Age group	At start	Now	At start	Now
	%	%	%	%
21–30	15	2	10	2
31–40	45	26	43	18
41–50	27	42	33	43
51–60	11	25	12	29
61 & over	2	5	2	8
Total	**100**	**100**	**100**	**100**

* *No recent figures are available for England*

The great majority of carers were now over the age of 40. The mean age of female carers at the time of the survey was 46 and at the start of fostering 39. That of male carers was 47 and 40 respectively. A broadly similar average for foster "mothers" was found by Bebbington and Miles in England (1990). The average age of female carers, however, disguises significant differences between carers living in different authorities. For example, whilst on average 27 per cent of carers were aged 41–50 in one authority, only four per cent were in this age group in another.

Household composition

Marital status
Almost four-fifths of carers were living as partners, mostly married, and the remaining fifth (21 per cent) were living alone at the time of the survey (see Table 4.2). With the exception of six single male carers, all the lone carers in this study were women. These figures compare with around 87 per cent of foster families in England being two parent (Bebbington and Miles, 1990). The researchers in the latter study refer to the under-representation of single carers. A number of authority variations were found in this present study concerning the recruitment of lone carers. For example, whilst 31 per cent of carers in one authority

were on their own, lone carers accounted for only 10 per cent in another. It is likely that a higher proportion of single carers will be found in England amongst minority ethnic communities.

Almost a quarter of married female carers and almost a fifth of male carers had been married before. The marital status of six per cent of carers had changed during the period of fostering with presumably significant consequences for the foster children. Half of these had divorced/separated, and about equal proportions of the rest had re-married or had been widowed.

Table 4.2

Status of carers at the time of the survey

Status	N	%
Couples/married	637	79
Single (never married)	35	4
Widowed	47	6
Divorced/separated	87	11
Total	**806**	**100**

Single carers

The majority of lone carers were divorced or separated from their partners. Only a few were widowed, followed by those who had never married. Four-fifths of all lone carers were now aged over 40, with almost half being over 50. Not surprisingly, perhaps, more single carers lived in flats than in detached or semi-detached dwellings, compared with those who were married. They were also far less likely to own their homes but lived in local authority rented accommodation and were less likely to have enclosed gardens. Similarly, few single carers kept pets, ran a car, or read a newspaper. Compared with couple carers, fewer single ones were working but more described themselves as retired.

Compared to couples, significantly fewer lone carers had own children living at home or had more than one child of their own. Though single carers had less space in their homes, they were more likely to foster slightly more children at any one time than other carers. They were also more likely to say that they 'never' thought of giving up fostering and that fostering met with their expectations wholly or partly. More important, they were less likely to specify the child's age group in advance.

The carers' own children

At the time of the survey, only eight per cent of fostering households had no children of their own. The others had on average three children per household, though not every child was living at home (see Table 4.3). The proportion of foster families with no own children contrasts greatly with the findings of the Gray and Parr (1957) study where 37 per cent were said then not to have own children. Bebbington and Miles (1990) explain this change in terms of the increased employment opportunities for women. One study has found that couples without their own children are the most successful at fostering (Dando and Minty, 1987). However, the Strathclyde study (1988) reported the opposite.

One in every ten carers reported that they had one or more adopted children (mostly one) and a similar percentage had one or more step-children. We think, however, that the number of step-children given and possibly of adopted ones too, was an underestimate. We contacted a number of carers to clarify their responses and we were told that some did not like the idea of singling out any of their children as "step-children". As the additional information did not cover everybody, the classification was not changed.

Table 4.3
Number of own children per household at the time of the survey (includes children who moved away)

Own children	All households N	Living away %
None	67	8
One	111	13
Two	221	27
Three	210	26
Four +	213	26
Total	**822**	**100**

Between starting to foster and now, an average of seven years later, few new children were born to the foster carers, suggesting that most families decide to foster after they have completed their families, a point also made by other studies (Parker, 1978; Keefe, 1983). It was also to be expected that at the start of fostering there would be more dependent children in each household, that is, 15 years old and under, than at the time of the survey (the age of 15 is the cut off point for dependent children used by the Registrar General). Almost three-fifths of own children were now 19 years old and over (for more details see table in Appendix B). The majority of younger carers had about two dependent children whereas most of the older ones had none or one.

At the time of the survey, a third of fostering households had no own children living at home and another quarter had only one. Three in ten households with female carers over 40 had no own children living at home which contrasted with just over one per cent for female carers under the age of 40. Whilst foster carers on the whole appear to have big families, when they foster they generally have fewer dependent children than the average household.

Self ascribed ethnicity

Over 99 per cent of respondents described themselves as white. The 822 fostering households surveyed included two couples who were Asian and five where there was an ethnic mix. At the same time, of the 24 (or two per cent) minority ethnic children who were fostered, 15 were said to be of mixed parentage; four Asian and five African-Caribbean. Two thirds of the latter children were fostered in all white households.

The proportion of minority ethnic people in Scotland described by the 1991 Census as Black, Pakistani, Indian or Chinese was around one per cent. In certain cities the proportion will be higher so that we cannot assume from the overall figures that minority ethnic carers are proportionately represented in all areas. Other studies summarised by Berridge (1997) highlight an overall shortage of foster carers from minority ethnic groups in England.

Religion

The great majority of respondents (62 per cent) indicated the mainstream Protestant Church as their religion. Around 17 per cent declared themselves to be Roman Catholic and almost one in ten were followers of other mainly Christian denominations, such as Baptist, Salvation Army and Mormons. The few Asian carers were either Muslim or Sikh. Somewhat more male than female carers declared no religion (16 to 12 per cent).

Religious faith did not feature much as a motivating factor to foster. However, a third of those who declared a religious affiliation described themselves as actively practising. This is still a higher proportion than the population in general, but there were substantial differences between areas. For example, around 50 per cent of carers in some areas were practising Christians, but only 5–10 per cent in some others. In 1993, over one in ten of those questioned for the British Social Attitudes survey said that they attended their church or meetings associated with their religion once a week or more. Carers with higher educational qualifications were more likely to be regular worshippers than those without.

Housing

Almost seven out of ten carers owned their homes (68 per cent) with a fifth living in local authority housing. This contrasts with only 51 per cent of home owners nationally (Census, 1991). Single carers, the very young (aged 21–30) and the older carers (aged over 60) were less likely to own their houses. The better qualified they were the more likely carers were to be home owners and to live in bigger houses. Overall, the typical foster carer's housing arrangements are that they own a semi-detached house with an enclosed garden and no more than three bedrooms. The majority of carers aged 41–50 had bigger houses with more than three bedrooms.

Health

The vast majority (95 per cent) of male and female carers described their health as good or very good, with almost 60 per cent describing it as 'very good'. Single women carers were more likely than women with partners to describe their health as poorer, as did females aged over 50. What is more puzzling is that significantly fewer young female and male carers aged 21–30 described their health as 'very good' than the rest. Unlike prospective adopters, carers do not have to have a medical but health is usually considered by social workers when doing the home study.

Other life style factors

The pattern of smoking in foster families

As smoking has become an issue in some authorities, we sought information on this topic from carers. Among both men and women, over a third said they smoked. This is slightly higher than the national Scottish average which, in 1994, was 28 per cent of men and 26 per cent of women. The proportion of households with at least one smoker was, however, considerably higher.

Table 4.4
The pattern of smoking amongst carers

	N	%
Both carers smoke	131	16
One carer smokes	353	44
No carer smokes	327	40
Total	**811**	**100**

Thus in 60 per cent of foster homes, at least one carer smokes. There was little indication that foster carers would accept the introduction of a 'no smoking' policy which some authorities, apparently, have been contemplating. Over a third stated that they would continue to foster if not allowed to smoke, but a broadly similar proportion indicated they would not. Only two per cent of those who smoked in Glasgow, in contrast to 49 per cent in Dundee, would be prepared to give up smoking for the sake of fostering.

Pets

Pets were included in the survey as an indication of the carers' interests and life style which could also help enrich some children's experiences.

Over three-quarters of the families (76 per cent) had a pet of some kind and half of these had more than one animal. Two-thirds of all carers had either a dog or a cat, compared to an estimated 52 per cent of all households in Britain.

Car ownership

Over 80 per cent of the foster families had a car. In 1993, 59 per cent of all households in Scotland had a car (Department of Transport in Social Trends, 1996) so that ownership among foster carers is much higher than the average. The national figures include the very elderly and young single people, so this may partly reflect life stage. It also reflects the fact that having a car is almost essential for transporting children to different schools, access visits, doctors, play groups, etc. Single carers and those aged over 50 were less likely to have a car than carers as a whole. As we say in a later chapter, claiming mileage allowance has become an area of frequent disputes between carers and authorities.

Educational qualifications

Only a minority of foster carers (17 per cent of men and 20 per cent of women) had remained in full-time education beyond the official leaving age. The proportion gaining 'O' grades and Highers is lower on average . than the educational level of the general population in 1992 (Social Trends, 1995). After leaving school, an equal percentage of female and male carers (29 per cent) had obtained qualifications. These were across the educational spectrum with the majority at vocational level. The better qualified were in the age group 31–50 and the least those aged 21–30, suggesting perhaps that carers gain qualifications throughout their lives.

Employment

Patterns of employment among carers varied widely. Overall, 72 per cent of male and 37 per cent female carers were employed. Of female carers working outside the home, 60 per cent worked part-time. Table 4.5 sets out the pattern of employment in families where there were two carers.

Table 4.5
Pattern of employment: two parent families

	N	%
Only male carer employed	242	38
Both carers employed	212	34
Neither carer employed	97	15
Only female carer employed	43	7
Both carers retired	39	6
Total	**633**	**100**

Even allowing for those who were retired, the 22 per cent unemployment rate among male carers was significantly higher than the national average then of nine per cent. The proportion was highest among men aged 51–60. These were followed by the youngest male carers aged 21–30. Variations across authorities were noted reflecting regional unemployment patterns. The more qualified female carers were, the more likely also they were to be working outside the home full-time.

Women aged 31–40 were the most likely to work outside the home and those least likely were aged over 50. Even where women were the sole earners, over half worked part-time. This could reflect employment opportunities, the demands of fostering, and the requirements of the placement authority. The diversity of employment patterns among foster families reflects trends in society as a whole. Only 38 per cent fit the traditional image of the woman caring for children at home while the man provides the family income outwith the home.

Occupational classification
Studies by Gray and Parr (1957) and George (1970) found foster carers concentrated in middle-class groups, whilst Adamson (1973, pp 109–127)) described fostering as 'traditionally working class'. Others have reported that the social class of foster carers was representative of wider society (Berridge and Cleaver, 1987; Rowe, 1984; Strathclyde, 1988; Bebbington and Miles, 1990). Keefe (1983) argued that the 'formidable' process of recruitment biases selection away from lower classes. Questions have often been asked about the impact of placing children

mostly from very disadvantaged backgrounds with 'middle-class' families, but one study found that 'fostering failure was no more the prerogative of certain social groups than others' (Berridge and Cleaver, 1987, p 145).

Using the Registrar General's Occupational Classification list, both female and male carers were grouped on a six point scale, distinguishing between manual and non-manual occupations. This was used as an indicator of social class.

Table 4.6
Classification by occupation of foster carers in Scotland*

Occup. classification Social Class	Female carers N	%	Scotland %	Male carers N	%	Scotland %
I -Professional	4	1	2	33	6	7
II- Managerial	144	27	28	155	27	24
III -Non manual	141	27	37	48	8	10
III -Manual	61	11	8	222	39	34
IV- Semi-skilled	150	28	15	93	16	17
V -Unskilled	33	6	10	21	4	6
	533	100	(100)	572	100	98

*A number of female carers (n.283) gave no previous or current occupation whilst others described themselves as 'foster carers', which was unclassifiable. A smaller percentage of men (n. 71) did not give their occupations either.

Starting with the female carers, there are a number of similarities and some differences when compared to the occupations of women as a whole in Scotland. For a start, compared to the national average, female carers in non-manual occupations (clerical, secretarial, administrative) were under-represented, but over-represented in social class IV (semi-skilled). Approximately the same percentage of women in social class II as in the general population foster. However, in one rural authority two-fifths of women fostering were classified as social class II compared to a national average of 28 per cent. In contrast, in another relatively prosperous authority there was only one carer from such a background.

Turning to the occupational classification of male foster carers, these are broadly in line with the occupations of the male population as a whole. Though the basis of the analysis is not exactly similar, nevertheless it does appear that more non-manual households in Scotland than in England are engaged in fostering (Bebbington and Miles, 1990). This may reflect fewer employment and other opportunities, especially for women in Scotland.

The following is a picture of the predominant occupations from which female and male carers were recruited:

Females	Males
• nursing	• Car/lorry/taxi drivers, postmen, security guards
• child minding	• small office and branch managers
• social work, teaching	• self-employed (shops, hotels, farms)
• care assistants/home helps and	• care workers, residential workers
• support workers	• skilled workers of any trade

Around two-fifths of female carers were connected with a social care sector job, including child minding and child nurseries. This is a higher proportion than the 23 per cent found in England (Bebbington and Miles, 1990).

SUMMARY

This chapter has described the background characteristics and life styles of foster carers and their families. Foster carers, on the whole, have stability and continuity in their lives. They are not different from others in the community except that as a group they tend to:
• be somewhat older than other parents with dependent children;
• be two-parent households;
• have somewhat bigger families but have significantly fewer dependent children compared to other households;
• start fostering after they finish child bearing;

- live in bigger houses, mostly owned by them and run their own car;
- have more pets;
- be active practising members of religious groups.

Where comparable figures are available there are few differences between foster carers in Scotland and those in England, except that more female foster carers in Scotland are:

- single;
- in non-manual occupations;
- connected with a social care sector job.

5   The recruitment of foster carers

In their review of the research literature of what works in family placement, Sellick and Thoburn (1996) acknowledge that research into effective approaches to recruitment is scarce. This chapter examines the arrangements and processes followed by authorities for the recruitment of foster carers, how carers hear about fostering, their stated motives for fostering, and why more people do not apply to foster.

RECRUITMENT STRATEGIES

Concern about the supply of foster carers inevitably puts the focus on recruitment and the retention of foster carers. Evidence about the scarcity of carers has come from many sources (Berridge and Cleaver, 1987; Shaw and Hipgrave, 1989; Coffin, 1993; Triseliotis et al, 1995a; Sinclair et al, 1995; Waterhouse, 1997). Not surprisingly, issues about the recruitment, supply and demand of carers were exercising almost all child care and family placement managers interviewed for this study.

The organisational systems for recruitment put in place by most authorities ensured a certain amount of coherence in the way the initial stages of recruitment, preparation and assessment were pursued. However, most service managers agreed that there was no overall and long-term strategy on recruitment and the general demand and supply of foster carers.

Recruitment campaigns, frequency, and methods used
Campaigns were mostly episodic. They were usually mounted when there was a pressing need, to coincide with the annual Foster Care Fortnight or at a time of year when experience had shown that they could be most productive. Campaigns could be all purpose ones, that is, for all types of family placement including adoption, and sometimes respite for children with learning difficulties, or focused solely on adolescents. There was

little multi-agency or shared recruitment except in one area to help cut costs. Some other authorities were beginning to think along the same lines.

Of 25 authorities answering this question, three-fifths had run a recruitment campaign in the last six months, five within the last year and another four within the last two years. One other authority said that it had ongoing recruitment. The study found no statistical relationship between the seriousness of carer shortages experienced and frequency of authority recruitment patterns.

What determined the frequency of recruitment campaigns
The predominant consideration that determined the type and frequency of campaigns run was budgetary, followed very closely by the availability or not of experienced staff. In a third of authorities both these factors were present. Budgetary limitations did not only affect the frequency and methods of recruitment used, but also the number of staff available to answer enquiries, visit those interested, and eventually carry out family assessments and preparatory work. As one placement manager observed:
> *Present staffing levels and workloads do not allow time for recruit-ment and follow up on any scale.*

Who organised and took part in campaigns
Placement service managers and their staff, mostly based in units, took the major responsibility for organising and taking part in recruitment campaigns. Where no such posts existed, the responsibility fell on the centre and/or the area child care team. Recruitment efforts did not always apparently permeate the whole agency and sometimes not even its child care section. Almost all the authorities said they involved their carers in organising and taking part in recruitment campaigns either 'regularly' or 'sometimes'. Carers themselves did not think that this went far enough.

How foster carers were attracted to fostering
Foster carers provided extensive information and comments on a range of topics concerned with recruitment. Table 5.1 summarises how carers first heard about fostering.

Table 5.1
How carers first heard about fostering

How heard	Responses	
	N*	%
Friends, relatives, through work, always knew	413	46
Newspaper article	169	19
Newspaper advertisement	148	17
TV and radio	97	11
Approach by department	26	3
Other	36	4
Total	**889**	

*These numbers refer to responses which exceed the number of carers responding to the questionnaire because more than one answer was allowed.

Word of mouth

Over half the current carers said they came to hear and learn about fostering through relatives and friends or through their work, especially in social care jobs. Some of these relatives and friends were themselves former or current foster carers. This form of recruitment possibly explains also why many carers were concentrated in certain streets, certain localities and even certain villages and towns, especially new towns. From the comments we had, it became obvious that the experiences of past and current carers are crucial in shaping a public image of fostering.

The press

The same table also highlights the power of the media and especially of the local press in raising awareness about child care need and fostering. Over a third of carers came to know about fostering either through reading a feature article or seeing an advertisement in the press, mostly their local paper. Around nine in ten fostering households regularly read a newspaper. One popular daily with its sister Sunday edition was read by over two-fifths of carers around the country. More important, over half of all carers read their local newspaper.

TV and radio

Television, and sometimes local radio, had played a significant impact on recruitment. With television, it was documentaries and sometimes advertisements that produced this effect. All but six per cent of carers said they watched television. ITV was by far the most popular channel, with twice as many watching this than BBC1. Almost one in seven carers said they often listened to the radio. Well over two-fifths of these (44 per cent) tuned into local commercial radio stations.

Poster displays, leaflets and stalls seemed to have had less impact but sometimes triggered off the final decision to do something about it.

A significant number of carers also described how an advertisement for a specific child brought them into fostering. A direct approach was occasionally used successfully by the fostering service to contact relatives and friends of a particular child who needed to be looked after. As a method of recruitment it could possibly be used more extensively than at present.

In their responses, authorities indicated the use of broadly the same recruitment methods as those that carers said had influenced them most. However, the national press was almost inaccessible to the many small authorities because it was too expensive for advertisements and negotiating feature articles seemed almost impossible. As with television documentaries, this was seen to be a central government responsibility. Though both television and local radio provided some free time to authorities during campaigns, this was not seen as enough and advertising was said to be beyond the means of most authorities.

Why more people do not come forward to foster

Current carers gave the following main explanations, in order of importance, of why more people are not attracted to fostering.

- Wide ignorance among the public concerning child care needs and fostering. Such wide ignorance was confirmed by Galbraith (1991) who asked people in Dundee about their knowledge of fostering.
- The apparent lack of confidence among many people of being able to do the job properly. Typical comments included: 'lack confidence', 'feeling not being good enough', 'being unable to cope with the demands', 'they think they do not have the capabilities required'.

- Protracted assessments or fears about not measuring up to agency expectations and of being rejected resulting in shaming. Potential carers might also think that they did not have the right background: 'not having the right job' or 'the right kind of house' or 'the right background', or 'being single' or 'living in partnership' or 'not being good enough'.
- Mistrust of social workers on account of their lack of credibility among the public and their perceived intrusiveness.
- The children's problems.
- Fears of accusations of wanting to make money out of children.
- Discomfort with the idea of returning children to their families.
- Lack of accommodation.
- Fears about false allegations of abuse.

These all add up to a low image for the children, social workers and the service. In many carers' views, some of the above issues and stereotypes could be more convincingly addressed by experienced carers than by professionals and, where appropriate, by young people and perhaps parents who have positive experiences of fostering. As some of them put it, 'we can answer questions from experience' or

Recruitment campaigns have to address both the vulnerability of children and the pressing need for foster homes.

Lowe (1990) found that using existing carers to network has been found to be successful, alongside advertisements in the press whilst the Strathclyde (1991) study reported fewer placement breakdowns where carers had undertaken this role.

The images of fostering portrayed during recruitment campaigns
Through an analysis of answers to the questionnaire and in subsequent interviews, the study put together the kind of images conveyed by authorities to the public during campaigns to address issues and stereotypes discussed earlier.

i) Welcoming interest from all sectors of the community

By stressing that fostering was open to all kinds of people, authorities were trying to encourage people from all walks of life to apply, irrespective of status, employment situation, the kind of job they held, where they lived or the type and size of house they had.

ii) Conveying a realistic picture about the demands of fostering

Service managers claimed to have tried in all their campaigns to convey a realistic picture of the demands and rewards of fostering, including the children's difficulties, even though the agencies' efforts may not always have been seen in that light by the public, including many current carers. The following is a typical comment made by managers:

Truthful about difficulties but balanced with the rewarding elements.

iii) Partnership, team work and the availability of support

Many managers said recruitment campaigns emphasised partnership, teamwork and the availability of support to children and carers with comments such as 'partnership, inclusive', 'working as part of a team', or 'well supported'.

No doubt the above are well-intentioned promises which are repeated during preparation and training. The same promises are also made in carers' manuals all contributing to raising the carers' expectations of the service. As we say in another chapter, a significant number of them came to feel disillusioned about these promises. Just as word of mouth can be a powerful recruitment medium, so spreading the word about unfulfilled promises could be damaging and off-putting.

iv) Emphasising local need

Though many current carers were prepared to foster children "in need" from any agency, almost half indicated a special commitment to their local services and local children. For this and other reasons, recruitment campaigns should be primarily local and then national in character. Some authorities were aware of this and emphasised local need in their campaigns. This was something that the new small authorities in particular were hoping to capitalise on by stressing that:

Our children need chances within our area.

Targeted needs and groups

Whilst authorities had some basic information on their existing carers, most had no accurate profiles on them to know who to target. This may account for the fact that recruitment campaigns traditionally have put most of the emphasis on the needs of the children and have less frequently targeted potential carer groups. The needs of adolescents have usually been centre stage. The fostering needs of children with disabilities were more likely to feature in special adverts than in campaigns. Many campaigns seemed also to put more emphasis on inviting applicants to become "permanent" foster carers or adoptive parents rather than for the other, more temporary forms of fostering which account for the vast majority of placements.

The great majority of authorities failed to target people connected with certain jobs such as social care, which attract two fifths of all carers. There was also no reference to targeting those aged 41–50, or even up to 55, who were identified by the study as being significantly under represented at recruitment but were undertaking some of the most challenging cases. Only occasional reference was made to single people, the unemployed and minority ethnic communities.

Recruitment messages also failed to put enough stress and provide clarity on financial matters and the financial rewards, thus perpetuating an apparent taboo of talking about money and perhaps reinforcing the notion that pay and caring do not go together. There was equally weak stress on the professional nature of the job and that fostering could be taken up as a career with the possibility of obtaining relevant qualifications.

Management attitudes to campaigns

Service and senior child care managers had mixed views about the value of recruitment campaigns. Campaigns were found to be costly to mount and, as a result, they were cautious about initiating them without evidence of results, preferably quick ones. Overall, a few managers were enthusiastic about campaigns, some cautious and many unconvinced. The enthusiasts were few, but they were convinced of the value of recruitment campaigns based on the results they had.

What was viewed as successful could also vary between authorities. One medium sized agency which selected seven carers from a single campaign described the result as 'poor', whilst another with similar results felt 'pleased'. It was claimed, by the cautious and unconvinced, that some campaigns would end up with not even a single enquiry. This made it difficult, it was said, to convince senior managers or councillors that campaigns provided 'value for money'. Several of the more successful authorities based their campaigns on:

- a good knowledge of their area and of their agency's fostering needs;
- working closely with experienced carers;
- having in place a well organised system for responding to enquiries and for a first visit, if wanted;
- involving children's social workers and their managers so as to identify with the recruitment efforts;
- using the local media;
- maintaining continuity.

(For more details on recruitment see Appendix A.)

RECRUITMENT AND FEARS ABOUT ALLEGATIONS OF ABUSE

Fears about false allegations of physical or sexual abuse by the foster children or their parents were in the minds of one in every four existing carers. Yet only three per cent thought this would stop other people from becoming foster carers. Fostering managers said that they had no evidence from their recruitment efforts that these fears were holding people back from applying in the first place. It was apparently after the matter was raised by the staff during preparation sessions that some applicants became aware of the implications and one or two decided to pull out. Exact numbers were not possible to gather as not everyone who withdraws gives the actual reasons for doing so.

MOTIVATION TO FOSTER

Our classification of the carers' explanations of what attracted them to fostering, which appear in Table 5.2 below, is based on their own accounts. It makes no pretensions of ascribing these to altruistic or non-altruistic, conscious or unconscious motives. Such motives are neither easy to recognise or categorise. Carers were simply asked to say what brought them into fostering. Though usually one or more key reasons were offered, in practice, the factors influencing the decision appeared complex, overlapping and difficult to separate or neatly package. In addition to the reasons put forward in the questionnaire, in interviews reference was made by a small number to recent losses of loved ones, mainly children, as a motive, There was a diversity of explanations offered but the following four stand out

- having something to offer;
- fondness/liking to care for children;
- awareness of need and wishing to offer something back to the community;
- Suits current family circumstances.

Personal, family or social factors and circumstances all appeared to have played a part in the decision.

Table 5.2
What attracted carers to fostering

Attraction	Female carer response		Male carer response	
	N	%	N	%
Have something to offer	290	38	164	30
Fondness for/liking of children	265	35	145	27
Awareness of need	163	21	106	20
Suits current family circumstances	130	17	39	7
Create/extend family	80	11	52	10
Children grown up/away	52	7	38	7
Financial	26	3	3	1
Own past experiences	22	3	18	3
Example of family	19	2	12	2
Wife's interest	–	–	70	13
Other	8	1	39	7
Total	**1,055**		**686**	

Something to offer

The most popular response was the conviction among many carers that they have something 'good' to offer to disadvantaged children, especially through their families and their way of life. This could be their home and its physical comforts, the experience of family life, love and the 'security' of home life. Some carers would say that they had 'a happy family', 'a secure home' or 'a comfortable home' or had 'a lot of love to give' and they would like to share these with children who were less fortunate than their own. They were enthusiasts for family life and were convinced that what they had to offer would be good for deprived or under-privileged children.

This kind of response allows us to speculate whether it is the more confident who are mostly attracted to fostering. Also whether it implies a superior way of life which would contrast with many of the children's backgrounds. If the latter, it may explain some of the difficulties and impatience this study found in the carers' relationships with the children's parents, which are discussed in another chapter. We also do not know whether such beliefs convey to the children certain negative connotations about their families, undermining their feelings of 'self-esteem' (see also Butler and Charles, 1999).

Fondness for children

The second most popular response was what carers described as their love, liking and concern for disadvantaged and vulnerable children. Caring for children, as they put it, was something they 'enjoyed' and 'liked', whilst also giving a child a home. It was not only 'good' for the children but also 'good' for the carers too. Within this group there was also a small number who mainly expressed their liking of looking after children, primarily for its intrinsic value to themselves. As some of them put it:

It gives me a feeling that someone loves me.

Or

A great need to satisfy my maternal instinct.

Only a tiny number, compared to the findings of Gray and Parr (1957) more than 40 years ago, were looking for a companion for their own child.

Awareness of need

A high proportion of carers referred to their awareness of child care need as the main motivating factor that brought them into fostering and their wish to 'give something back to the community':

You cannot stand by idly in the face of so much need.

Suiting own family circumstances

A significant proportion of the responses (17 per cent) came from those, especially female carers, some single, who said that fostering suited their current family circumstances. These were carers who wanted 'to be at home' or 'to work from home' so as to be with their own children or because it suited them. Though their explanations were pragmatic, there was no indication that this was a wholly self-regarding activity:

. . . providing a loving environment for children whilst at home with my own.

Family creators/family enlargers

A powerful motive was the wish of a significant group of carers who came into fostering either to create a family or enlarge an existing one. They used words such as: 'the desire to have a family', 'to have children around' or 'I always wanted a big family'.

Others missed their children who moved away from home and wanted also to put their parenting skills into some 'good' use:

We do not like a quiet house, so we thought fostering would be "good" for us.

Other attractions

Whilst religious beliefs were rarely mentioned, carers were more likely to worship, compared to the rest of the population. More surprising was the 13 per cent of men who said that they came into fostering because of their 'wives' interest' or 'to please their wives'. The idea of adoption through fostering featured much less than was found in the Gray and Parr (1957) study. Furthermore, this seemed to be encouraged more in some authorities than others. Carers who adopted were also very likely to cease fostering, at least for the time being.

Only a small group of carers (three per cent) openly said they came into fostering because of their own past experiences of having been fostered or having had a very depriving experience. According to Dando and Minty (1987) an identification with the needs of deprived children seems to be a key factor that attracts carers to fostering.

Time between deciding to foster and applying

Only just under a third of foster carers made enquiries within a month of deciding they would be interested in foster care. Overall, around three out of every five started the process within three months of their decision and another fifth between 4 and 12 months.

In the majority of cases (52 per cent) it was the female carer who initiated the decision to foster. In 44 per cent of cases it was a joint decision, and in the remaining (4 per cent) it was the male carer's. With only a couple of exceptions, those who had children old enough to understand said they had consulted them. Most of them said they had even consulted older children who had left home many years ago. Many older children living away were said to offer a lot of support to their parents, viewing fostering as a family affair.

SUMMARY

- In around half the authorities, formal campaigns were held back because of budgetary constraints and non-availability of experienced staff.
- Almost half the authorities had held a recruitment campaign in the last six months of the study. Placement staff took most of the responsibility.
- A lot of effort went into recruitment but mostly in an episodic and unsystematic way. What appeared to be missing were a long-term policy and direction, clear targeting and a marketing approach.
- The expectation for 'instant' results influenced the way some managers viewed such efforts.
- Campaigns focused mainly on the specific needs of children and were less well targeted to particular groups of carers, such as the over 40s who are currently significantly under-represented at recruitment; also

single people, those employed in the social care sector, the childless or child free and the unemployed.

- Word of mouth, feature articles and advertisements in the local press and documentaries on TV appeared to be the most influential recruitment methods.

- Foster carers come into fostering with a range of motives, mostly altruistic, and only in a minority of cases could these be viewed as self-regarding. Many of them also come into fostering at a time when it suits their domestic circumstances and leave when these change.

- On the whole, foster carers are confident that they have something to offer; have a commitment to disadvantaged children; and have a heightened sense of awareness about child care need.

- Powerful factors that apparently hold other people back from applying include lack of awareness, fear that they do not measure up to agency expectations, lack of confidence to care for other people's children, mistrust of social workers, the poor image of children needing care, having to return children to their families and protracted assessments.

- Two-fifths of authorities said that they regularly used experienced carers in recruitment campaigns, but this was not seen by many carers to go far enough. They maintained that their much greater involvement could help bridge the apparent credibility gap between social workers and the public and better address some of the misconceptions and stereotypes held about fostering.

6 The assessment, preparation and training of foster carers

The purpose of this chapter is to identify the authorities' procedures from the time of receiving initial enquiries by prospective carers to the process of assessment, preparation, approval and training.

STAGES USUALLY FOLLOWED FROM ENQUIRY TO APPROVAL

All authorities, with some variations, followed the recruitment stages set out in the figure below.

Figure 6.1

Stages from enquiry to approval

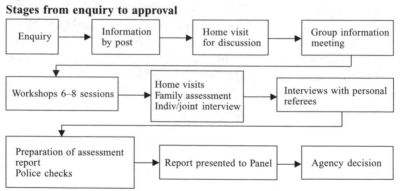

Responding to enquiries

Eight out of ten authorities said they had written procedures on how to respond to enquiries from would-be foster carers. The rest said they were developing them. Three out of every five authorities also said that they were able to respond to enquiries with information within three days and another quarter within a week. The amount of time it took authorities to respond to enquiries or pay visits was found to be unrelated to whether they were experiencing serious shortages of carers or not.

There was agreement that, in some authorities, campaigns were not always well co-ordinated between central and area teams which were meant to respond to enquiries. As a result some confusion could arise about the point of first contact and enquirers could be asked to ring other numbers.

Existing carers were, on the whole, positive about the initial response they had had and particularly the offer of an early individual meeting to discuss fostering. An agency's commitment to children was often judged by these early responses. Obviously we do not know about the views of those who did not proceed to apply or who were not finally approved. Table 6.1 summarises the approaches that carers found helpful and unhelpful.

Table 6.1
Satisfactory and unsatisfactory responses to enquiries

Satisfactory	Unsatisfactory
A helpful switch-board reception	An off-putting or indifferent switch-board response
Speaking to someone knowledgeable	No-one appearing to know who carried responsibility to provide information
Information posted quickly	Asked to phone again because person responsible unavailable
Being offered an early chance of face--to-face meeting/discussions	Uninformed discussion on the phone and/or getting evasive replies
Talking to an experienced carer	Material not arriving by post
Attendance at open meeting, if desired	Face-to-face meeting not offered or being cancelled
Application form provided	Not being offered the choice about attendance at open meetings
	Prolonged procedures

Most of the visiting staff were found by carers to be courteous, knowledgeable and informative, thus creating a very good impression of the service. Comments were made such as: 'very responsive and prompt', 'quick response' or 'information was sent quickly and a worker came round within two days'. Opportunities to meet and talk to an experienced foster carer were particularly valued. The following comment summarises the process at its best:

Very satisfactory. Intelligent information on the phone and information sent quickly. Somebody else came round very quickly to tell me more about it and discuss it.

Overall, there seemed to be a good fit between the processes that carers found satisfactory and the systems set up by the majority of authorities for responding to enquiries. Centrally based units were better placed for directing all enquiries to a single point, compared with arrangements where a quick response was not always possible.

ELIGIBILITY CRITERIA

Almost half the authorities (15) indicated that they had one or more eligibility criteria (see Table 6.2). A few said that they were applying the same criteria as in adoption. This disregards the substantial differences between fostering and adoption, and such confusion must inevitably be conveyed to the public and the carers selected.

Table 6.2

Type of exclusion criteria operated by authorities

	Age	Marital Status	Gay men	Lesbians	Work	Smoking	Other
N.	9	1	5	5	7	8	6

Age

Around a quarter of the authorities had minimum and maximum age criteria. The stipulations usually were for people not to be under 21 or over 60. Sometimes the minimum age was 25, especially for those interested in taking adolescents. The age of 60 could be seen as rather low considering that the average life-span is in the middle seventies and that many couples are delaying having children.

Marital status
Only one agency indicated that it had eligibility criteria about the marital status of applicants, but no explanation was offered as to what this meant.

Gay men and lesbians
Scottish authorities are bound by the legal requirements which exclude lesbians and gay men from living *together* and acting as foster carers. Gay men and lesbians can foster, provided that they are 'living and acting alone'.

Work requirements
A fifth of authorities had some kind of requirement about work. They expected that either at least one partner in a relationship would stay at home or that the carers would be available after school hours or to show that they had 'enough time for the children's needs'. Some carers, as the study found, made a conscious decision to foster older children so that they could go out to work and be available after school hours.

Smoking
A quarter of the authorities had a criterion about smoking, usually that no carer who smoked would be allowed to foster very young children. One agency, however, would offer smokers medical counselling (see Chapter 4 on carers' smoking patterns).

Other
Under 'other' criteria signifying eligibility, six authorities included having dangerous animals, convictions, especially against children, and health issues. One agency had 'mandatory' training as a requirement.

THE FAMILY ASSESSMENT, PREPARATION AND TRAINING OF CARERS

Within authorities there was a fair amount of blurring between family assessment, preparation to foster and pre-fostering training. Where the one stopped and the other began was often hazy.

The family assessment of carers
All authorities had in place arrangements for the preparation and assessment of carers. Criteria used to assess the suitability of new applicants included their social and personal circumstances, life styles and household composition.

In three-fifths of authorities the assessment of carers was carried out by placement workers based in units. Only in two authorities was this the exclusive responsibility of area team social work staff. In the remaining authorities (30 per cent) it was undertaken by a combination of placement workers and area team fieldworkers. In the case of couples, the home study usually entailed both joint and individual interviews. The majority of authorities also allowed for time when they would meet the children of the family. Usually about six meetings were scheduled to take place every fortnight or at longer intervals. During the same period fostering staff would take up medical and other references.

Our attempt to establish whether carers were involved in the assessment of new carers proved rather unsuccessful as only eight authorities answered this question. Two of these said 'regularly', two 'sometimes' and four 'never'. As seen in various parts of this study, carers did not think that authorities involved experienced carers sufficiently in all the processes associated with recruitment, preparation and training. It was also very rare for children and young people who had been fostered, for birth parents or the carers' own children to play a part in the same processes.

Carer reactions to the home study/assessment
Current carers' reactions to the assessment were favourable and they had a lot of praise for the staff involved. Certainly the assessment was only rarely experienced as 'inquisitive', 'tactless', 'insensitive' or 'intrusive'.

Even, as one put it, 'asking about our childhood experiences was all right' provided 'they didn't go on about it'. With few exceptions, most liked the idea of groups and of separate and joint meetings with their partners and sometimes the involvement of their children.

Current carers valued the 'sensitivity' with which questions were asked and recognised the reasons why these had to be asked. Again the study did not obtain the views of those who withdrew or were not accepted. Nevertheless, a lot of the sting seems to have been taken out of the process of assessment by new approaches which are task centred with the focus on explanation and sharing, along with preparatory workshops taking place (see Triseliotis *et al*, 1995a). A study by Cambridgeshire County Council (1990) also reported that those who foster were generally satisfied with the recruitment and approval process.

The preparation of carers

Within authorities there were different views as to what was meant by 'preparation' and whether it should be part of the family assessment and, if so, at what point it should take place. Most carers interviewed by the study thought that preparation, with social workers present, was a form of assessment, irrespective of how it was presented.

Another blurring was that between preparation and training before beginning to foster. In some authorities these became synonymous. All the authorities had schemes for the preparation/training of prospective carers before they started to foster. The approach was mostly based on group sessions, and occasionally on a combination of group and individual meetings or simply of individual meetings. Around half the authorities expected attendance at group meetings to be compulsory whilst others recommended the groups 'strongly'. Exceptions or modifications to the requirement were mainly made for applicants from rural areas.

The use of workshops and groups for the preparation and training of foster carers has now become an established and almost uniform practice across the UK. Only four authorities indicated they were not using groups, mainly because they were small and new carers were attracted on an individual basis. Some of the same authorities, along with several rural ones, had adapted the themes used in group preparation in ways that could be used with individuals and couples. Besides group/individual processes, some authorities would use one or more half or whole day seminars. The contents of pre-fostering preparation provided a combination of sharing of life and family experiences, educational input, exploration of motives and discussion of the fostering tasks.

There was a consensus amongst current carers that assessment and preparation/ training often took too long. They could understand a period of around four months but anything beyond that was seen as unnecessarily too long. The following is one of a number of comments:

The home study process took about a year. The social worker visited often. It seemed protracted.

Only a few authorities were able to complete assessments and the approval of carers within the four month period that carers saw as 'reasonable'. The majority, however, completed them within a six month period. Fostering staff were not in favour of reducing the length of time below the six month period because of the time required for preparation, delays in police checks, obtaining references and the non-availability of staff.

The continued training of carers

Most carers greatly valued both pre-placement training and the continued forms of training offered by their authorities. Only a small minority put total faith in their own experience. There was also a lot of praise for the organisation and delivery of training, but inevitably many carers also found shortcomings, which they explained as resulting from cuts to the training budget. Another factor was the continually changing nature of the task with more things needing to be learned. The needs of foster children, changes in social conditions, new legislation and new requirements, imposed new demands on carers and they expected training to respond more quickly, and to be more coherent and more relevant.

Most carers attached great importance to continued training. All authorities said they provided some form of continued training for their carers but its frequency, pattern and content varied. However, one in every six carers said they were not provided with continued training.

Only a quarter of authorities said that training was compulsory, mainly for those carers fostering for special schemes for adolescents. On the whole there was lack of a clear strategy with regard to the training and continued training of carers. Much reliance was placed by all authorities on the support groups acting also as training groups. Like many carers, managers referred to continued training as being: 'periodic'; as having 'no cohesion'; 'erratic'; 'no pattern'; 'variable' or 'irregular'.

In authorities covering long distances and in the Island authorities, the usual pattern was to hold annual and bi annual events lasting one or more days, along with occasional periodic half-day sessions One authority had linked part of its fostering training to a local college and several others were encouraging their carers to apply for vocational qualifications.

Attendance at training and support group sessions
Of those carers provided with continued training, just over one in ten never attended either training sessions or support groups. There was a close overlap between those not attending training and those not attending groups. Those drawing a fee were more likely than the rest to attend training and groups regularly. Female carers aged 21–40 with less than five years fostering experience were the least likely to attend. As we found, the latter group had more child care responsibilities than others and more of them also worked outside the home.

Attendance at groups did not differ significantly between those authorities who made it compulsory and the rest, or between urban and rural areas. In one city agency, though, almost all its carers attended regularly. Of those who attended support groups, there was overwhelming approval for what the groups offered. Almost all those who attended groups enjoyed them. They liked hearing particularly about the fostering experiences of other carers, sharing problems and exchanging information:

> In the groups a good balance is maintained between theory and the how of doing things and socialising. The groups are always with the social workers present, but much also depends on the individual social workers.

However much many carers liked their placement workers who took responsibility for organising and running most group sessions, the majority view was that staff were also 'over-controlling' the groups, sometimes by their sheer presence. Many wanted more opportunities to meet by themselves, with carers acting as convenors.

When carers started their own group the department took it over and it flopped.

Continued training

According to carers, and many managers, what has been missing from much continued training was greater coherence and continuity. Carers made reference to many issues that featured under "preparation", but which they thought required more detailed coverage later including:

- Understanding the nature of fostering, roles and expectations. The children's fostering needs and the interface between fostering and residential care, child minding and adoption.
- How the social work department is organised and how it operates, including the place of fostering within it.
- The emotional impact of fostering on carers and their families.
- Routine care (physical, hygiene, HIV/AIDS, safety in the home).
- Understanding about child development, attachment and separations and about the circumstances that bring children into the system and foster care.
- Skill enhancement for the handling of difficult behaviours in children, including drug and alcohol abuse.
- Understanding and helping children who have been sexually and/or physically abused.
- The legal context of fostering and the operation of the children's hearing system.
- Dealing/working with birth parents and managing contact (the input so far was mostly viewed as inadequate).
- How to let children go.
- Coping with and managing abuse allegations.
- Expectations, rights and responsibilities of everybody involved in fostering including children's rights, carers' expectations of social workers and the agency, the place and role of parents and the idea of contracts.

- Clarity on financial entitlements.

The above seems a formidable list, but then the task itself is complex and so are the children's needs. Understanding and managing children's difficulties, including children who have been abused, was very high on the carers' list. Equally high on their agenda were 'how to let children go' and 'dealing with natural parents and managing contact'.

How well the carers were prepared or trained

Along with the provision of post-placement support, preparation and continued training are seen as contributing to the greater stability of the placement (See Berridge and Cleaver, 1987; Triseliotis, 1988 and 1989; Sellick and Thoburn, 1996). Six out of ten carers felt either prepared or well prepared, three out of every ten felt 'neither prepared nor unprepared' whilst one in ten said they had no preparation. As expected, there were wide variations between authorities with 53 per cent of carers in one authority feeling well prepared compared to 14 per cent in another.

For the satisfied ones, besides learning from training, there were also opportunities to meet staff and other carers with whom more lasting relationships were developed. These proved invaluable at times of crises. For most, presentations and discussions with experienced carers were the highlight of preparation, but apparently this was not done often enough. More interesting was the finding that carers who felt prepared were less likely to say that they found the children difficult or they often or sometimes felt like giving up. Lowe (1990) claimed that preparation was often far from adequate and was a major reason for placement breakdown.

A major criticism, though, was of authorities not preparing them better on how to manage sexual abuse, the children's problems and parental visits, or how to let children go. There were also serious criticisms of authorities for not being fully 'honest' and 'truthful' about how disturbed some of the children were or how 'demanding' and 'stressful' fostering could be.

Some of the carers fostering children with disabilities claimed that preparation and training did not usually address the needs and management of such children. As a result, some found themselves unprepared for the task and had to find out for themselves. In addition, some carers found the visiting social workers equally lacking in expertise on the subject and so carers were unable to get the support they felt they needed. Within carers' groups, disability was marginalised and some carers would have preferred the opportunity to meet, at least occasionally, with other carers and families who were looking after similar children to benefit from each others' experiences.

Figure 6.2
How prepared carers felt to foster their first foster child

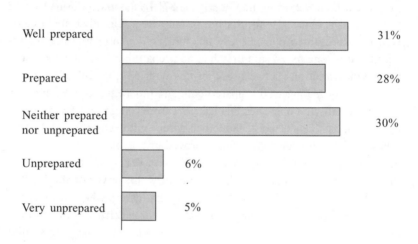

SUMMARY

- Almost all authorities used well developed, systematic and standard-ised procedures for answering enquiries, carrying out the family assessment and the preparation and training of carers. Gaps found were mainly the result of staff shortages and poor co-ordination. It could be surmised that the low annual withdrawal rate reported later is partly due to these improved methods.
- Three-fifths of carers felt 'well prepared' or 'prepared'. Those who felt like this were less likely to say that they found the children

difficult or that they often or sometimes felt like giving up.

- Groups were highly enjoyed and so was input by experienced carers.
- Carers drawing a fee were more likely than others to attend both training and groups.
- Over three-fifths of carer assessments were undertaken by link workers and most of the rest jointly with area child care teams. Seven in ten assessments were completed within a six month period.
- Too much blurring surrounded the stages and timing of family assessment, preparation, training, support groups and of continued training.
- Carers suggested closer links between pre and post-approval training with much greater emphasis on the continuity and coherence of training, preferably leading to a qualification for those who want it.

7 Supply and demand

This chapter makes use of official and other statistical information obtained by the study to present an overall picture on the supply of and demand for foster carers. It also reports on an analysis of material from a census survey on the demand for foster carers. Comparisons with the situation in England are made where appropriate or available.

CHILDREN IN FOSTER CARE OVER THE YEARS

Table 7.1 shows how, over the past 30 years, the proportion of children fostered under the Boarding Out Regulations in England and Scotland has been changing in relation to all children in care/looked after away from home. Of the 10,678 children in care in Scotland in 1967, 59 per cent were shown as being boarded out. This contrasted with 50 per cent of the 66,200 children in care in England and Wales for the same period. By 1974, the number of all children in care in both Scotland and England and Wales rose sharply, whilst the number and proportion of those in foster care dropped equally sharply. From 1980 onwards, we see sharp drops in the number of all children in care/looked after in both countries and a corresponding increase in the proportion (not numbers) of those fostered. Since then, however, the proportion of those fostered in England and Wales has been consistently higher than in Scotland. As an example, by 1997, the proportion of children fostered in Scotland rose to 50 per cent (or 2,708, children) whilst in England it rose to 65 per cent (or 33,400 children). It is possible, however, that the proportion of those fostered in England is exaggerated by the recent inclusion of all children looked after by relatives and friends, instead of only those looked after by approved carers, whether non-relatives or relatives and friends.

Table 7.1

Children in Scotland and England and Wales formally fostered as a proportion of all in care/looked after away from home between 1967 and 1997*

Year	Scotland			England**		
	All in care	Fostered	% Fostered	All in care	Fostered	% Fostered
1967	10,678	6,300	59	66,200	33,100	50
1974	1⅃,⅃1⅂	5,661	46	91,300	29,400	32
1980	8,749	3,264	⅃⅃	95 300	35,200	37
1990	5,774	2,553	44	60,500	⅃⅃,⅃⅃⅃	57
1997	5,336	2,708	50	51,600	33,400	65

*Sources: Scottish Office Annual Statistics on Children in Care/Looked After away from home; Home Office (1967); Department of Health Annual Statistics on Children in Care/Looked After.

**Until 1989 statistics of children in care in England and Wales were presented jointly. Since then they have been disaggregated.

Figure 7.1

Children fostered in Scotland and England in relation to all children in care/looked after

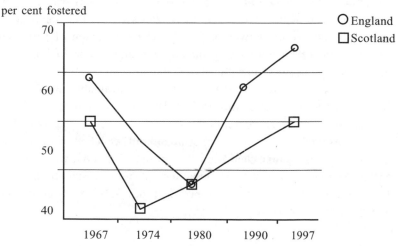

Source: Annual Reports of Children in Care/Looked After (Scotland) (England)

79

On the whole, the fluctuations in the proportion of children in foster care can be mostly attributed to the rise and fall of all children in care/ looked after away from home. However, the number of children fostered over the years in England, as different from the percentage, has remained much more constant than in Scotland. As an example, the number of children fostered in Scotland in 1997 was less than half of those fostered in 1967, whereas the English figures remained almost the same.

The relationship between numbers in care and the proportion in foster care over the years is illustrated in Figure 7.1.

THE NUMBER AND DISTRIBUTION OF FOSTER CARERS

Whilst official statistics indicate the number of children fostered, they do not give the number of carers or of new recruitments and losses each year. Precise figures on the number of foster carers in England are not available but estimates put it at around 23,000 fostering households (see Table 7.1). Of these, at least 2,707 (or 12 per cent) are relatives and friends. Some 450 additional fostering units were provided by the voluntary/ independent sector (Waterhouse, 1997).

Based on returns from all Scottish authorities we found that, at the end of March 1997, there were 1,923 approved households who were fostering non-related children and managed by local authorities. Local authorities had also approved another 226 carers (or 10 per cent of the total) who were relatives or friends. The percentage of approved relative foster carers in both England and Scotland was uneven between authorities. Some Scottish authorities had none whilst half of one small authority's carers were related to the children. No doubt authorities in both countries place more children with relatives and friends but do not approve them as foster carers.

After excluding the 17 per cent of households which at any one time are not used, on average each Scottish fostering household was found to foster 1.5 children. It is estimated that the number of foster children per household in England went up from 1.3 in the 1950s to 1.8 in the late 1980s (Bebbington and Miles, 1990).

Table 7.1

Foster carers in Scotland and England fostering non-related and related children for local authority and the voluntary/independent sector*

Type of agency	Non-related N	Related N	Vol/Indep. N	Total N
Local authority (Scotland)	1,923	226	54	2,203
Local authority (England)*	20,293	2,707	454	23,454

All numbers for Scotland refer to the year ending March 1997. The English figures refer to the year 1994 (Waterhouse, 1997).

In both England and Scotland, around one household in every 1,000 foster but there are very wide variations between authorities. For example, in Scottish rural authorities the average per household is one in every 700 but is only one in every 1,600 for urban areas, where most child care need is to be found. New Towns proved to be fruitful areas for recruitment purposes. Carers living in New Towns were also found to be more likely to foster for a special scheme.

On average, authorities in Scotland recruited one female carer to every 400 of all women aged 30–44 compared to only one for every 1,100 of all women aged 45–59. The overall under-representation of the latter age group suggests that there is scope for targeting this age group much more than at present. As we say later, carers in the age group 41–50 undertake some of the most demanding forms of fostering and are also among some of the most satisfied.

As far as it could be ascertained, the proportion of foster carer households each agency had was unrelated to the way the fostering service was organised or to budgetary constraints. However, the lowest recruitment occurred mainly in authorities where carers disagreed or disagreed strongly that their social worker was available when needed.

Proportion of children fostered by authorities
At the end of March 1997, around half the children looked after away from home in Scotland were placed with approved foster carers but the

81

proportions varied considerably between authorities. Whilst several authorities had over 80 per cent in foster care, almost a quarter had less than 30 per cent. The big differences were mainly attributed to the way the boundaries of the new unitary authorities were drawn. Disparities between English authorities were less pronounced. The highest proportion of children placed in foster care by a single authority there was 86 per cent and the lowest 46 per cent, with the average around 65 per cent.

Rural authorities in Scotland had the highest percentage of children placed (63 per cent) followed by semi-rural ones at 44 per cent and urban ones at 41 per cent. The overall semi-urban percentage was depressed by a single authority which managed hardly any foster carers. Similar figures by geographical location are not available for England, but differences there between unitary authorities, metropolitan districts, shire counties and inner and outer London boroughs were insignificant (Department of Health: Children Looked After by Local Authorities at 31.3.97).

Out of boundaries placements
Around one in every ten carers in both England and Scotland were managed by authorities outside their home boundaries. Wide variations existed between authorities. A quarter of all placements managed by one Scottish authority and 91 per cent made by an English one were outside their boundaries. City authorities in Scotland and inner based London boroughs had the highest proportion of carers outside their boundaries (Waterhouse, 1997).

SHORTAGE OR OVER-SUPPLY OF CARERS?

Authorities in all areas stated that they were experiencing shortages in all areas, but the most serious ones were urban authorities in Scotland and county councils in England. Seven out of ten Scottish authorities said they were experiencing 'some' foster carer shortages, a quarter 'serious' shortages and only one had a surplus. Broadly similar serious shortages were experienced in the placement of similar types of children in both countries, especially the placement of older children. Compared to Scottish authorities, English ones reported that they experienced more difficulties in recruiting for children with difficult behaviours, children with disabilities and minority ethnic children. Some placement managers in Scotland were keen to point out that the real problem was not so much with single characteristics of individual children but when character-istics, needs and circumstances overlapped such as older age, challenging behaviour and a complex family situation.

Table 7.2

Percentage of local authorities in Scotland and England* reporting serious carer shortages by type of children's need

Older children		Sibling groups		Ethnic minority		Long term placements		Difficult behaviour		With dis-abilities		Certain localities	
Sc. %	Eng %	Sc. %	Eng %	Sc. %	Eng %	Sc. %	Eng %	Sc. %	Eng %	Sc. %	Eng %	Sc. %	Eng %
68	72	48	68	46	61	45	38	45	63	32	65	32	38

* Waterhouse, 1997

RECRUITMENT AND LOSSES OF CARERS

Specific figures on the recruitment and losses of foster carers for England are not available. Table 7.3, however, contrasts English and Scottish authorities which stated they had gained or lost carers over a one-year period. Proportionately within a one-year period, Scottish authorities seemed to have made more gains than English ones. The growth in numbers was most evident among urban authorities in Scotland and among metropolitan ones in England.

Table 7.3

The proportion of authorities who gained or lost carers*

Country	Gained %	No change %	Lost %	Total %
Scotland	75	9	16	100
England	51	29	20	100

*Figures for Scotland refer to 1997. English figures are for 1994 (Waterhouse, 1997).

A more detailed analysis shows that around a quarter of authorities in both Scotland and England recruited within a year more than 20 per cent of their carer stock and, for almost three-quarters, carer losses were under 10 per cent.

Table 7.4

Proportion of authorities who recruited or lost carers in relation to all their carers and above or below certain percentage points

Country	Recruitment of carers			Loss of carers		
	Over 20%	*10–20%*	*Under 10%*	*Over 20%*	*10–20%*	*Under 10%*
Scotland*	22%	50%	28%	3%	28%	69%
England*	29%	44%	27%	4%	21%	75%

*Scottish figures are for 1997. English figures are for 1994 (Waterhouse, 1997).

The overall annual losses of carers of under 10 per cent for both Scotland and England are lower than expected. They contrast with the high numbers of carers leaving the service reported by Cliffe and Berridge (1991) which is possibly explained by the fact that their numbers were based on a study of the practices of a single authority. As we have found there can be wide variations between individual authorities. Without underestimating the importance of retention, the main conclusion that can be drawn from both the Scottish and English figures is that the retention of carers is not a major problem for the majority. Rather the need is for more recruitment. It could be claimed that the attention paid over the last 15 or so years to the preparation, training and support of carers has been paying dividends.

Enquiries, applications and approvals

Table 7.5, based on Scottish figures since no specific figures are available for England, illustrates the relationship between enquiries, firm applications, number of carers approved and numbers lost. The 32 Scottish local authorities received 2,518 enquiries during the period 1.4.96 to 31.3.97. Of these, only 493 (or 20 per cent) resulted in firm applications (see table). Of the 493 firm applicants, 290 (59 per cent) went on to be selected/approved as carers. (It is possible that some applicants were still under consideration at the time the returns were made.) Whilst some authorities selected one in every three firm applicants, others selected them all. This suggests considerable variation in selection procedures resulting mainly from the pressure for placements.

Table 7.5

Number of enquiries, firm applications and approvals and carers lost between 1.4.96 and 31.3.97

Enquiries	Applications		Approvals		Carers lost	
N	N	% of enqs.	N	% of applics.	N	% of all carers
2,518	493	20	290	59	155	7

A SNAPSHOT OF DEMAND FOR PLACEMENTS

As part of the Scottish study, a census survey was conducted on demand and supply covering a six-week period in September and October 1997. Thirty of the 32 authorities participated. The main purpose of the census was to establish the demand for different types of fostering placement and how the demand matched with the supply.

The demand for placements

During the six week census period, front-line staff in the 30 authorities made between them 916 requests for fostering placements, but 163 (or 18 per cent) were withdrawn before placements were found. The main reasons for the withdrawals included alternative arrangements having been made with parents, friends or relatives or a residential resource. This left placement/link workers to find foster homes for 753 children. Almost two-fifths of these children had been referred before and the rest were first referrals. Six per cent of all the requests were from one agency to another.

Assuming the pattern of referrals remained constant, it would result in around 8,000 children in Scotland being referred annually for foster placement. If the same proportions held true of England, it would result in around 80,000 children being referred for placement in a single year.

Age, sex and sibling status of children requiring placement

The 753 referrals requiring placements were about equally split between male and female children. Children under six, between 6 and 11 and 12 and over, were all represented in broadly similar proportions to their coming into care. One in every ten of those referred were over the age of 14. Of all referrals made, almost two-fifths were members of sibling groups with half of these being of three or more siblings. There were some, but not many, variations between authorities in the proportion of different age groups referred for placements.

Table 7.6
The age group and sex of children referred for placement*

| Sex | 0–2 yrs | 3–5 yrs | 6–11 yrs | 12+ | Total |
	%	%	%	%	%
Male	15	18	36	31	51
Female	16	15	30	39	49
Total	**15**	**17**	**33**	**35**	**100**

* *The ages of 19 children are missing.*

The children's needs

Of the 753 children referred for placement, 404 (or 54%) were said to have some special need (Table 7.7). The predominant one was the display of emotional/behavioural difficulties, followed by school problems, offending and disabilities. It can only be assumed that, for the rest of the children, the circumstances that necessitated the need for placement had to do more with the parents' circumstances than their own. There was reference on the forms to parental short-term illness, general neglect and/or inability to cope at times because of alcohol and/or drug abuse. Children presenting learning difficulties, physical disability and health problems accounted for around one in every ten referrals.

The proportion of members of sibling groups who were said to display emotional, behavioural, offending or other difficulties was around half compared to those of the non-sibling group. We can only surmise that a significant proportion of members of sibling groups were needing foster care for reasons other than those connected with their individual behaviours or disability. This may also explain the later reported and surprising finding that placements for sibling groups were somewhat easier to find than for others.

Table 7.7
The children's special needs*

Emot/ Behav. %	School assoc. %	Offending %	Physical disability %	Learning disability %	Other %
46	17	7	6	5	8

* In some cases more than one special need applied, so percentages do not add up to a hundred.

Expected length of placement

The fostering literature, as well as research, suggests that all plans for children should specify the length of time a placement is meant to last because this also largely influences the expectations, roles and relationships of the participants (Berridge and Cleaver, 1987; Rowe *et al*, 1989; Triseliotis *et al*, 1995b). For over a quarter of referrals, it was unknown for how long the placement was expected to last. In some authorities this applied to as many as half the children, while in others this was true of one in six. Where the expected length of placement was unknown, children were less likely to go to a first choice placement.

For around two out of every five firm referrals, the request was for a placement that was meant to last for under four weeks. However, all of one authority's requests during the census period, and three-quarters of another, were for placements to last for under four weeks, which contrasted with only 17 per cent in a third authority. Respite and short-term placements were extensively used by authorities as a relief service to parents and children, other than those with learning difficulties. For example, for over a third of children aged 12 and over, the placement was expected to last for less than four weeks.

Emergencies or planned

Over half the children (55 per cent) were referred as emergencies and the rest as planned. First referrals were more likely to come in as emergencies than cases known beforehand. In one agency almost all the 100 or so referrals during the period of the census were made as emergencies. Another large urban authority placed many children referred as "emergencies" for up to six weeks, until a longer term placement was found. We do not know how many of these children, if any, exceeded their six week "emergency" placement.

Was the child placed or not?

Just over seven out of ten children were placed within the specified census period but the rest (28 per cent) remained unplaced. (The census period was extended by a fortnight to allow for late placements, but not for new referrals.) In some authorities the rate of unplaced children was much higher, e.g. 10 out of 12 referrals made to one small agency remained unplaced and 16 of 24 made to another. Applied nationally, and assuming that some of the children would not eventually be placed, this would result in no foster placements being found for over 2,000 children annually in Scotland and for 21,000 in England.

Of those children placed, almost half were placed on the same day as they were referred for placement and 70 per cent within one week. A fifth of all children were delayed for more than two weeks. There was no evidence that children who went to other than first choice placements were unnecessarily delayed in being placed.

The children who were not placed within the period of the census

The main groups of children most likely to remain unplaced in order of frequency were:

- children from minority ethnic backgrounds;
- those requiring long-term care, though some of the delay could be related to more lengthy planning on their behalf which fell outside the census period;
- offenders;
- older children;
- children with disabilities;

- those displaying emotional/behavioural problems and school problems;
- sibling groups.

First choice (preferred) placements

In view of earlier studies suggesting that, because of the scarcity of placements there is a tendency for children to be placed where there is a vacancy rather than where they are ideally suited (Rowe, 1984; Berridge and Cleaver, 1987), we were surprised to find that, of those children for whom placements were found, around six out of every seven were said to have gone to placements considered first choice. Those under the age of three and over 15 were more likely to go to a first choice placement. The proportion of siblings going to other than first choice placements was double that of other groups, reflecting their splitting. Authorities said they tried to keep siblings within easy distance of each other if they were split.

Figure 7.2 presents the full picture. Overall, two out of every five children were either not placed or placed in a placement that was not a first choice. Urban areas had the highest percentage of unplaced children in relation to their total number of carers.

Figure 7.2
The relationship between referrals and placements made

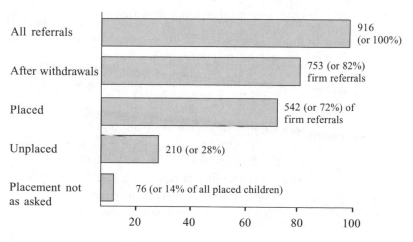

SUMMARY

- Depending on whether those staying with relatives and friends who have not been approved as carers are included, between half and two thirds of children in care/looked after away from home in Scotland and England now live with carers.
- The proportion, as separate from the number, of all children in foster care has been fluctuating over the last three decades. Numbers in foster care in England, compared with Scotland, have been holding better over the last three decades. Since the early 1990s, though, there has been a small but steady rise in the number as well as the proportion, of all children fostered in Scotland.
- At the end of March 1997, there were 2,203 accredited fostering households in Scotland, compared to an estimated number of 23,000 in England. In both countries around one in every 1,000 households foster, but significant variations exist between authorities. Similarly, significant differences were found between authorities in the recruitment of carers with different characteristics, such as age and status.
- Each fostering household fosters a mean number of 1.5 children at any one time.
- Unlike Scotland, where most serious shortages were experienced in the big cities and other urban areas, in England this was mainly true of county council authorities.
- A surprising and encouraging finding was the low percentage of carers lost to the service each year in both countries (under 10%). Though there should be no complacency, the problem for both countries is not so much the retention of carers as new recruitment. In Scotland, recruitment was found to be higher than losses by six per cent, but much more needs to be done.
- Based on census figures from Scotland, the number of children referred for foster placement during a twelve-month period is likely to amount to 8,000 in Scotland and 80,000 in England. Two-fifths of these will be members of sibling groups. Over half the children are likely to display emotional or behavioural problems.
- Over half of the children were referred as emergencies.

- Two-fifths of the placements were meant to last for less than four weeks and another 13 per cent for less than three months, but for almost three in every ten, the length of the placement was not known.
- A sign of the service's strength is that of those children placed; almost half were placed on the same day as they were referred for placement.
- Nearly three in every ten children could not be placed within the period of the census because of the lack of placements. Overall, two out of every five children were either not placed at all, or went to a placement which was not a first choice. Of those placed, six out of every seven went to a first choice placement.
- A composite picture emerging from the census figures and the authorities' perceptions indicated that serious placement shortages exist for the following groups of children: minority ethnic; displaying problems; older; requiring long-term placement; sibling groups; and those with disabilities.

8 The experience of fostering

After identifying the types of fostering undertaken and the kind of children fostered, this chapter looks at how carers experience looking after the children, including the best and worst aspects of fostering, and whether their expectations in relation to fostering were met or not.

TYPE OF FOSTERING UNDERTAKEN

Trying to identify the type of fostering each carer was undertaking at the time of the survey proved difficult and elusive. Some of the confusion was related to the fact that each authority used different terms to describe the length and nature of essentially similar types of fostering. The absence of a shared terminology is unlikely to encourage inter-agency collaboration and may cause misunderstandings and confusion. Most confusion was between medium and long-term placements. Whilst the classification of carers may be undesirable, that of placements is essential, because it partly determines expectations and sets roles for subsequent work.

Using standard length categories, by far the most common form of fostering now undertaken was of a short-term nature i.e. under three months (40 per cent). This covered short-term, respite, emergency and pre-adoption placements. It was followed by medium-term foster care i.e. up to two years (30 per cent) and then long-term i.e. indefinite (28 per cent).

Special schemes

Overall, one-third of all foster placements were said to be part of a special scheme. There were two main types of such schemes: those for children with a learning or physical disability (8 per cent of all fostering households) or those taking adolescents/teenagers (26 per cent of all placements). Besides the basic maintenance allowance, all those fostering for a special scheme were drawing, as a kind of reward, either a fee or an enhanced allowance which could be up to double the basic maintenance allowance. Yet whether carers were designated as part of a special scheme or not sometimes depended on the route through which the child had been referred to the placement team. Whilst this seemed to operate as a form of rationing, affected carers raised questions about the equity of the system that allowed this to happen. This also explains why more households appeared to care for an adolescent or a child with a disability than were involved with 'special schemes'.

Special schemes for adolescents/teenagers

These schemes, which covered the fostering of what were felt to be particularly challenging and difficult adolescents/teenagers, carried different names in different authorities. The most common was 'community caring'. Around a quarter of all households (26 per cent) were fostering adolescents/ teenagers as part of a community care scheme. Belonging to a 'special scheme' did not preclude carers from taking other types of children. Compared to the average, some authorities had double the proportion of community carers, whilst some others had none or were well below the average.

LENGTH OF FOSTERING EXPERIENCE

Just over half of the current carers in Scotland had been fostering for five or fewer years. A quarter of these had been fostering for two years or less and 12 per cent of them for a year or less. At the other end, a quarter had been fostering for 11 or more years and five per cent of them for over 21 years (Figure 8.1). There were wide variations between the authorities featuring in the sample concerning the average number of years their foster carers had served. (No comparable English figures are available.)

The average length of fostering experience for carers was seven years (s.d. 7). Differences were found between authorities, with one where the average in this authority was nine years whilst in another it was only three. Were the average length to go up by a third, it would significantly reduce the need for new recruitment. Research on fostering breakdowns suggests that increased experience in fostering is associated with significantly lower breakdown rates (Berridge and Cleaver, 1987).

Figure 8.1
Years of fostering experience

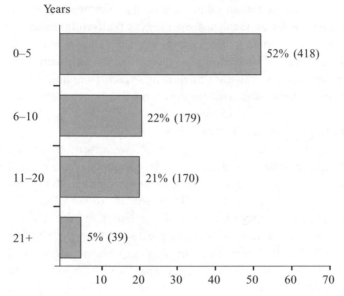

Note: Not known: 16

CHILDREN FOSTERED

On average, each carer had so far fostered 18 children (s.d. 33; see Table in Appendix B), but again there were wide variations between authorities. Around two-fifths of carers had fostered five or less children, but a similar proportion had fostered between six and 30. Some 12 carers had in fact each fostered more than 150 children. The large numbers mostly represent short stays and sibling groups.

Most households fostered 1 or 2 children at a time with an average of 1.5 children each. Excluding vacancies, almost half of all households were fostering one child, while almost one household in five (18 per cent) was fostering three or more children, in most cases sibling groups. Bebbington and Miles (1990) reported that in England almost 50 per cent of households were fostering more than one child but the writers made no reference to vacancies. The number of children fostered at any one time made no difference to the levels of carer satisfaction with the operation of the fostering service.

The fact that almost a fifth of placements (17 per cent) were not taken up was mostly due to the absence of suitable children to match the preferences of carers or the placements were not where they were needed most. No doubt, having a number of placements on hold should promote better matching, except that the preferences of many carers without children were mostly for under-five-year-olds whereas most of the need was for older children. In other cases the vacancies were too distant from where the child lived.

Sex and age group of foster children

Table 8.1 sets out the age group of the children fostered at the time of the survey.

Table 8.1
Age group of foster children

Age group	Age of children fostered				
	0–4	5–9	10–15	16+	Total
	%	%	%	%	%
Scotland	19	26	43	12	100
England*	21	23	42	14	100

Department of Health: Children Looked After by Local Authorities, year ending 31.3.1997.

Just over half (53 per cent) of the children were boys and 47 per cent girls. The age groups of children fostered in Scotland and England do not differ significantly. The children were also largely representative of all looked after children. Almost a fifth of all the children in foster care were under the age of five. Another quarter or so were aged 5–9, but the great majority, ranging between half and three-fifths, were ten and over. Around eight in ten children in Scotland were in households where the female carer was aged over 40. Male and female children were placed in similar proportions in each age group.

Children with disabilities

One in every six carers was fostering a child with a disability but only half of them belonged to a special scheme. As expected, there were variations between authorities, ranging from 32 per cent of carers (i.e. fostering a disabled child) in one to none in another. Over half of these children were said to present learning difficulties, sometimes accompanied by some physical disability. Physical disabilities accounted for 38 per cent of the children in this group. Physical conditions included mainly hearing and sight impairment and occasional foetal alcohol syndrome. One in ten of the children in the group with disabilities were described as having more than one disability.

Sibling groups

Just over a fifth of households (22 per cent) fostered a sibling group, most commonly of two children. Over a third of one city authority's placements involved sibling groups compared to only one in ten of a rural authority. There is now considerable research evidence about the advantages of placing siblings together (see Mullender, 1999; Triseliotis, 1989).

Ethnicity

Two per cent of the children fostered in Scotland were described to be black or of mixed ethnic origin. The majority of these were of mixed parentage with the rest being Asian or Afro-Caribbean. We could not find comparative figures for England. Like in Scotland, a great number of authorities in England reported serious shortages in placements for children of minority ethnic backgrounds (Waterhouse, 1997).

Fostering related children

Based on returns and official statistics, it is estimated that around one in ten of all looked after children in England and Scotland lives with relatives and friends acting as approved foster carers (Deptartment of Health, 1999; Scottish Office, 1999). A broadly similar proportion in Scotland were found to be looked after by relatives and friends informally.

FOSTER CHILDREN AND CARERS

Almost half the carers who had placements (48 per cent) indicated that they found the children they were *currently* fostering more difficult than they had expected. The problems, in the carers' view, made it difficult to handle the children, discipline them, care for or relate to them. Carers also found boys somewhat more difficult than girls. Minnis (1999) reported that 60 per cent of the children in her foster care study had behaviour problems.

The age or fostering experience of the female carer made no difference to finding the foster children more difficult than expected, unless the experience stretched for more than 20 years in which case they did not find them more difficult than expected. The expectation also that those caring for adolescents/teenagers would find the children more difficult was not borne out. Possible explanations include the view that children of all age groups are likely to display serious problems because of the type of child now coming into the system; that those caring for adolescents and teenagers come prepared for difficulties; and, as we found, those acting as community carers seemed to get more attention from the fostering services and were less critical of them.

Finding the children more difficult than expected, however, was associated with

- having a poor relationship with the agency;
- feeling less well prepared;
- support being perceived as low; and
- unavailability of the social worker.

The vast majority of the problems identified (74 per cent) had to do with the behavioural and emotional difficulties displayed by the children. Behavioural problems included accounts of aggression and destructiveness, the fear of attacks, the use of abusive language and sometimes young people running away. On the emotional side there were descriptions of soiling and smearing, bed-wetting, failure to respond, being difficult to relate to or causing self harm.

The management of the difficulties was often found taxing and frustrating, raising a mixture of feelings including frustration, inadequacy or of being misled by the agency. In the carers' view, some of the children were very 'disturbed' as a result of repeated separations, rejection and sometimes serious abuse. In addition, the children lagged behind in their education and social behaviour. There were many complaints by carers about insufficient information on the children's backgrounds and difficulties that, if supplied, could have enabled them to understand and handle the problems better. Carers maintained that knowing about the children's backgrounds and difficulties enabled them to respond much more appropriately, a point borne out by research (Barth and Berry, 1988).

Some of the problems and their management made carers feel at times 'useless' and 'inadequate'. Not surprisingly a common request was for more training on the management of behaviours. This was also an area in which more support and help from the children's social workers and from outside would have been welcomed, they said. When it came to managing children with disabilities, carers again expected more support, including respite and relief. Promises about this were not, apparently, always kept.

From the carers' accounts, it also appears that there may be unacknowledged differences between them and social workers in the way they approach the management of problems displayed by the children. As an example, the social work approach was interpreted by some carers as 'indulgence', 'siding with the child', 'softness', 'not paying much attention to what the carers had to put up with' or simply 'undermining' the authority of the foster carers.

RESPITE FROM FOSTERING

Breaks, or respite, are different from gaps between placements, in that they are purposely built into the placement arrangement. Differentiating between respite and holidays was not easy because formal respite arrangements were infrequent. Six out of ten carers indicated that they had no break from fostering in the preceding year. Around a third took at least one break, with six per cent having taken 2–3 breaks and one per cent more than three. Again there were many variations between authorities. Almost two-fifths of carers said that they would not like a break even though about a third of them had never had a break before. For some, it seemed to be a matter of pride not to be seen to be needing a holiday or break.

One-fifth of those who took a break did so when there was a gap in placement. At the same time, carers did not like to have big gaps between placements as their whole financial arrangements were upset. Some carers preferred to take the fostered children with them on holiday, either because it was not practical to find respite for them or they did not like the idea of leaving younger children behind.

Two authorities, one of which specialised in the placement of children with disabilities, had schemes which allowed for respite or an annual holiday, but these were not apparently always implemented or some carers were unaware of their availability. In the absence of clear contractual arrangements, some carers were uncertain or had mixed feelings about raising the issue of respite. Whilst some were definite that breaks and respite should be part of the contract, for a significant minority it was not seen as important. As already hinted at, even carers who would like to see breaks as part of a contractual arrangement did not like the possibility of leaving the foster child with other carers or in a home, unless it was with a carer with whom they had developed reciprocal arrangements.

The most common explanation offered by over half the respondents for taking a break was the need to take a holiday with their families. Many said that they 'owed' it to them, with or without the foster children. Around a third indicated that the decision was the result of stress and tiredness brought about by fostering and/or a very demanding placement. Family circumstances, such as illness, birth of a child and bereavement accounted for almost a quarter of other explanations given.

A need for respite/holiday was not always associated with length of fostering experience or number of children being cared for or with the child's age. Sometimes carers who had fostered only for six months, or had fostered only one child, indicated the need for a break. On the other hand, some long-standing carers would say that there was no need for respite.

FOSTER CARER INVOLVEMENT

Information summarised in Table 8.2 shows that, with the exception of recruitment and training, and participation on Panels, the regular involvement of carers in the authorities' fostering activities in both Scotland and England was infrequent. Carers were least involved in the review of other carers, complaints against other carers, and as members of management groups. The low level of carer involvement in many activities largely confirmed the carers' views. Rural and semi-rural authorities in Scotland were less likely than others to involve their carers in most of the activities outlined, possibly because of geographical factors.

Table 8.2

Proportion of authorities regularly involving their carers in a number of activities

Activity	Scotland %	England* %
Recruitment	63	65
Training	60	70
Supporting other carers	35	50
Reviews of other carers	–	5
Panel membership	30	70
Complaints against others	3	9
Management groups	3	13
Working parties	19	35
Children's plans	29	15
Annual reviews of the service	24	12

* *Waterhouse, 1997.*

BENEFITS AND ATTRACTIONS OF FOSTERING

Foster carers responding to the questionnaire took the opportunity to provide extensive comments on what they perceived to be the main benefits and attractions of fostering for themselves and their families. Their responses are classified in Table 8.3.

Table 8.3
The benefits and attractions of fostering (Scotland)

Benefits	N	%
Seeing children progress	230	28
Sense of achievement	206	25
Job satisfaction	166	20
Enhancement of our lives	135	16
Insight into other people's problems	78	9
Doing something worthwhile	77	9
Children returning to see us	41	5
Response to a challenge	22	1
Working from home	12	2
No benefits	13	2
Other	31	4

Apart from 13 carers out of the 822, who could see no benefits at all, the rest outlined fostering's attractions for themselves and their families. Top of the list of benefits was 'seeing children progress', 'a sense of achievement', 'job satisfaction' and not far behind 'enhancement' of the fostering household's lives. There are many obvious overlaps between these four benefits.

Seeing children progress and doing something worthwhile
It may be thought only common sense that if concern for children was a key motivating factor which brought many carers into fostering, then equally seeing the children do well would be seen as fulfilment of their motives and a justification for their actions, including the hard work and effort they put into it. There were many positive comments on this and the following is typical:

To see a child blossom and gain confidence from a normal family life.

A particular pleasure for many carers were 'hugs' and 'smiles' and returned love from the children. These encouraged many not to give up fostering and persevere in times of crises. Apart from making them 'feel good', positive experiences also helped to reassure them that they were doing the right thing.

Sense of achievement and job satisfaction

Closely allied to seeing children progress and do well was the associated sense of achievement, making it feel 'worthwhile' as many put it. There was satisfaction from being able to help a 'troubled' child build 'trust and security'. Alongside this went a sense of 'fulfilment', an enhancement of 'self-worth' for achieving something, and an increase in 'self-confidence' arising from something 'well done':

Feeling you were able to make a difference.

Finding resources I was unaware of.

A number of carers, especially those who saw themselves as 'professional' and 'doing a job', felt satisfaction and took 'pride' and 'pleasure' from seeing that the job was well done:

. . . job well done and knowing that I had a hand in a successful outcome.

Other carers singled out the satisfaction of working at home whilst also doing a 'worthwhile' job. Less frequently they also stressed the importance of pay going with the job which enabled them to stay at home:

It allows me to earn a small income while doing a "job" which I enjoy and find rewarding.

Enhancement of life

A significant number of carers perceived the benefits of fostering as extending to the whole family, having 'enhanced' their lives, 'enlarged our relationships' or made us 'more tolerant' as people. They used phrases such as 'fulfilment as a family', 'gave us a purpose in life', 'made many new friends through fostering'. The following is a typical comment:

There has been more happiness in our home.

Other perceived benefits included learning a lot about children and oneself, being kept active or kept informed and up-to-date about schooling, new technology and child development or gaining insight into 'other people's lives', meaning the children's families.

Though only indirect reference was made to community approval, this was sometimes implied in statements about neighbours being 'full of praise' or neighbours saying that this is 'something we could not do', conveying admiration for those who could do it. These attractions also provide some clues as to why most carers persevere in the face of many adversities and frustrations.

THE WORST ASPECTS OF FOSTERING

When carers were asked to describe the worst aspects of fostering, 707 (86 per cent) offered a number of descriptions and explanations. It is useful to be reminded of their own repeated comment that fostering is 'very hard work', 'very demanding' and, by its nature, 'very stressful'. It was not inconsistent for the same carers to describe both the benefits of fostering and its worst aspects. Furthermore, knowing about the draw-backs makes it easier to do something about them.

Table 8.4
The worst aspects of fostering (Scotland)

Worst aspect	N	%
The operation of the fostering services	200	24
The children's problems	166	20
Hard work and stress	162	20
Nothing	115	14
When children leave	86	10
Feeling inadequate	63	8
Parental visits	56	7
General invasion of privacy	42	5
Children failing	41	5
Allegations	30	4
Other	37	5

The three drawbacks that came top of the list were the operation of the fostering services; the children's problems; and hard work and stress.

Other important explanations offered included the 'pain' when children leave; feelings of inadequacy for not being able to help some very 'disturbed' or 'troublesome' children; parental visits and behaviour;

the general invasion of privacy; false allegations of abuse; and low finance. Other concerns included cutbacks in resources; anxiety and fear of a child being hurt whilst in their care; making a wrong decision about a child; and again the possible long-term impact of fostering on their own families. Finally, 14 per cent said that there were no 'worst' aspects in fostering.

ALLEGATIONS OF ABUSE

Only four per cent of carers named fear about 'allegations of abuse' as one of the worst aspects of fostering. In answer to another question about possible worries concerning the future of fostering was the fear of false allegations. There was an abundance of comments such as: 'fear of allegations', 'false allegations', 'coming under suspicion', or 'there is no way to protect yourself against allegations'.

Allegations and complaints about abuse could come in two forms: either against carers or a member of their household, or against a foster child for abusing a member of the fostering household. Three main kinds of allegations and complaints were identified in relation to foster carers:

- serious abuse (sexual or physical);
- heavy-handedness on the part of a carer; and
- incompetence, neglect, or misbehaviour e.g. drink problem.

The 32 Scottish authorities had between them a total of 2,149 carers. Table 8.5 shows that, during the period under study (1.4.96 to 31.3.97), the authorities had 75 allegations of abuse made to them affecting 3.5 per cent of all fostering households. Eight of the authorities had no allegations made either about sexual or physical abuse. Of the 75 allegations made, 28 (1.3 per cent of all carers) were about sexual abuse and 47 (2.2 per cent of all carers) were about physical abuse. Twelve carers (0.6 per cent of all carers) were de-registered as a result of allegations, six for each of the two categories of abuse. In one case the agency concerned was awaiting the decision of the court before considering de-registration.

Overall, while allegations of physical abuse were higher than those of sexual abuse, nevertheless it was more likely for a sexual allegation to end in de-registration than one involving physical abuse. Around one in every 20 active carers said they had recently been the subject of allegations of abuse.

Table 8.5

Allegations of sexual and physical abuse made against carers during the period 1.4.96 to 31.3.97 and number of de-registered carers

Sexual abuse		De-registered carers		Physical abuse		De-registered	
N	% of all carers	N	% of all carers	N	% of all carers	N	% of all carers
28	1.5	0	0.1	47	2.6	6	0.3

Procedures for dealing with allegations

Eight out of ten authorities had written guidelines and procedures on the handling of allegations and about support to carers during this period. However, in many authorities new procedures were being developed because of dissatisfaction with existing ones. Some of the current procedures were described as 'insensitive', 'heavy-handed', 'inconsistent' or as 'surrounded by ambiguity'.

Much uncertainty, it was also claimed, surrounded the kind of support that could be made available to carers during the period of investigations, and that not enough had been done to help carers understand the existing procedures.

Depending on the nature of the allegation made, a choice would be made between three possible forms of action: invoking child protection procedures in serious cases; setting up an internal inquiry for allegations such as 'heavy-handedness' or 'incompetence' on the part of a carer; or dismissing the allegations without an investigation but looking into it at the annual review. Child protection procedures would be invoked mostly for allegations of sexual or physical abuse. These did not differ from any other child protection investigation with police involvement. Authorities relied heavily on the advice of the police on how to proceed, especially with regard to the continued involvement of staff with the carers. If allegations were proved, then they would certainly lead to de-registration. De-registration following internal inquiries would depend on the seriousness of the allegation or its repetition.

A frequent complaint by carers who had been involved in allegations was the absence of support and the amount of time it sometimes took for an internal inquiry to be carried out, keeping them in a state of continued anxiety. Carers who had been involved in false allegations experienced them as very distressing and did not find the procedures satisfactory either. Some said: 'it came as a shock' or that they 'felt isolated' or 'unfairly treated' or 'deserted' or 'abandoned by the agency' or 'did not know what was going on'.

DID FOSTERING MEET WITH THE CARERS' EXPECTATIONS?

We asked female and male carers to indicate separately, towards the end of the study, whether fostering had met with their expectations or not.

Around half of the female and male carers said that fostering did meet with their expectations (Table 8.6); Two-fifths said 'partly so' and the rest, one in ten, said it did not. There were no big differences in the responses between female and male carers. Single carers were more likely to say that fostering met their expectations, or at least partly so, whilst those aged 31–40 were least likely to. The average for all authorities of those who said 'no' was 10 per cent, but in a couple of authorities it was down to three per cent and in others up to between 20 and 25 per cent. Though on the whole partners gave the same answer as each other, there were a few exceptions with one partner saying 'yes' to the question and the other 'no'.

Table 8.6
Has fostering met with your expectations?

Level	Female carer		Male carer	
	N	*%*	*N*	*%*
Yes	406	52	280	49
Partly so	299	38	230	40
No	77	10	61	11
Total	**782**	**100**	**571**	**100**

Of those carers who indicated that their expectations had not been met, around a quarter said they found the work much harder than they had expected. A broadly similar proportion found the children more disturbed than expected, while nearly one-fifth found the operation of the fostering services disappointing. The responses again indicate the importance of carers getting a more realistic picture of the demands of fostering without exaggerating them and of providing much more training and support around children's difficulties.

SUMMARY

- The most common form of fostering found was a combination of emergency, short-term and respite care. This was followed by medium and long-term.
- Each household was fostering on average 1.5 children at any one time, and had fostered for an average of seven years, suggesting a fair amount of continuity.
- Carers foster for an average of seven years but wide variations were found between authorities in how long they could hold onto their carers.
- Many carers felt overloaded by difficult children and increased demands. Almost half the children displayed serious behavioural and emotional problems presenting challenges to their carers' abilities and skills. Carers did not always obtain the kind of support they would like to help them manage the difficulties.
- Finding the children more difficult than expected was associated with: having a poor relationship with the agency; feeling less well prepared; support being perceived as low; and unavailability of the social worker.
- Only a minority of authorities had built respite arrangements into their contracts with carers.
- The regular involvement of carers in the agency's fostering activities fell short of the carers' expectations.
- The great majority of carers found fostering hard and demanding but also rewarding. Nine in ten stated that their expectations of fostering were either fully or partly met.

- Almost four per cent of all fostering households in Scotland were involved in sexual or physical abuse allegations over a one-year period. De-registration affected 0.7 per cent or about one in every 140 carers.

9 Children who foster

This chapter concentrates on the interaction between own and foster children as perceived by foster carers.

BACKGROUND

Fostering is associated with children joining and leaving families. In the process there are opportunities for company, closeness and friendships as well as for rivalry and rejection. As others have also pointed out, the family unit is like a very finely balanced 'mobile' and a new member, such as a foster child joining or leaving, could unbalance the functioning of the whole household (Pugh, 1996). The re-establishment of the equilibrium and of reasonable stability, following such an experience, cannot always be guaranteed. In systems terms it imposes boundary permeability and even boundary loss because of the comings and goings by the foster children, their families and the social services staff.

Existing family members, besides having to make space for the newcomer, will also have to reach, implicitly or explicitly, a new understanding over such matters as the operation of rules, the allocation of roles and the distribution of power, so as to take account of the presence of the new arrival. Much can also depend on how well the respective children are prepared for the change. An American study claims that a crucial issue is the allocation of parental time between own and foster children. Also, tensions can arise about differential treatment with some own children saying that their parents were stricter in applying the rules with them while allowing the foster children 'to get whatever they wanted' (Poland and Groze, 1993).

It is only in the last ten or so years that the impact of fostering on own children has been looked at from the children's perspective. The few studies available have been small scale with mostly less than 20 children being interviewed and even fewer parents. Nonetheless, these have identified some very important concepts alerting policy makers and practitioners to issues requiring attention. In a small scale study, Thoburn (1989) found that only half of the 'home grown' children in the study were satisfied following the arrival of a permanently placed child. Another study by Part (1993) found that 80 per cent of own children interviewed stated that they liked fostering, while the remainder had more mixed views (15 per cent), with four per cent not liking their family to foster. Pugh's (1996) study confirmed Part's findings. The best thing about fostering identified by own children in both studies were:

- companionship,
- looking after babies and young children and
- the challenge of helping.

Some children in Pugh's study felt ignored or that they missed their mother's attention or were simply seen by social workers as part of the foster child's environment, with little or no attention paid to them. Participants in the two studies wished there was more systematic and consistent preparation of the children, more background information made available and more involvement both at the start and later. On the same theme, Martin (1993) adds that 'the carers' children felt they had not been taken seriously or listened to, and that their own needs to be prepared for the demands of fostering had not been, and were not being met' (p 17).

Another study which looked at families fostering children with severe disabilities found that around a quarter of the family's children expressed strong concerns. Most of the dissatisfied were girls and much of the dissatisfaction seemed to arise from having to undertake caring tasks in relation to the placed children (Reed, 1993). The researcher added that in all but one of these instances, the young person placed with the family was relatively close in age and that the daily lives of these young women had been significantly altered by the placement.

Caplan (1988) too raised some disquieting aspects, this time concerning the psychological impact of fostering on own children. His pilot study in the USA was based on interviews with 15 own children aged 6–12 and found that parents assumed above average maturity on the part of their children, so tending to minimise the impact of fostering on them. Furthermore, own children conceptualised fostering as involving children who were abandoned by their parents because they were bad and consequently expressed to the researcher ideas and fears of they themselves being abandoned by their parents.

THE PRESENT STUDY

A reminder: at the start of fostering just under two-fifths of foster carers reported that their own children were under ten years old, almost a quarter (24 per cent) were between the ages of 10 and 15 and the remainder (39 per cent) over 15. The possible impact of fostering on their families was at the forefront of many respondents' concerns, especially those with dependent children. Studies suggest that when foster carers perceive that their own families and children are suffering as a result of fostering, they are likely to give up (see Von Arnim, 1988; Wilkinson, 1988; Triseliotis *et al*, 1998). Data from a small scale study by Lemieux also show that 'dissatisfaction with the foster child was first voiced by a biological child, then followed by the foster child's removal' (Quoted by Poland and Groze, 1993). Carers in our study expressed fears about abuse or allegations of abuse, the possibility of own children receiving less attention from their parents or learning 'bad' habits from the foster children. As one parent put it:

It can affect your own children if you don't take time to ask them if there are any problems for them. We can forget they can have problems with the placement.

Explaining to the children and involving them in decisions was seen by some as one way of reducing possible adverse effects.

Fostering is a family task and without the support of your own children it cannot be done.

SLEEPING ARRANGEMENTS

In the past, the significance of sleeping arrangements was usually related to space and privacy. More recently, concerns about sexual abuse have brought additional complications (see Utting, 1997 and Kent, 1997 reports). As a way of reducing this risk, and also providing greater privacy to the children, some authorities have been considering the introduction of a policy requiring each foster child to have his/her own bedroom. No doubt the children's safety comes first, but such a policy will inevitably put further strain on recruitment, especially of younger carers with less space in their homes.

Table 9.1 shows that around two-thirds of the foster children were found to have their own room, one in every seven shared with another foster child (sometimes a sibling) and one in every six shared with one of the carers' own children. Foster children were more likely to share bedrooms with the carers' own in younger fostering households who had less space in their homes compared to other age groups.

Table 9.1
Sleeping arrangements for the last or current placed child

Place	N	%
Own room	520	63
Shares with another foster child	125	15
Shares with own child	136	17
Not relevant/no reply	41	5
Total	**822**	**100**

THE CARERS' EVALUATION OF THE IMPACT OF FOSTERING ON THEIR CHILDREN

Most of the foster carers with dependent children at the time commented on the perceived impact of fostering on their children. These descriptions were classified and are set out in the next table.

Table 9.2
Overall impact of fostering on own children as seen by carers

Impact	%
Positive	32
More positive than negative	30
Mixed	21
More negative than positive	15
Negative	2
Total	**100**

Around three out of every five carers saw the impact of fostering on their children as positive or as more positive than negative. Just over a fifth saw it as mixed and almost another fifth as negative or more negative than positive. These figures are somewhat more negative than those reported by Part (1993) based on her interviews with own children.

a) Positive or more positive than negative experiences

The majority of carers were at pains to convey the positive impact that fostering, in their view, had on their own children and how it helped especially to mould their character beneficially. Perhaps some of these carers underestimated their children's fears as Caplan (1988) indicated. Below is a summary of the benefits of fostering as seen by parents in this study and as seen by children in two other studies. The parents put the emphasis on learning through the experience, while the children put it on their enjoyment from it. Some of the children's more individual comments, though, confirmed the parents' observations on the themes of social awareness and on how more fortunate they were than others.

The parents' view (this study)	The children's view (Part, 1993; Pugh, 1996)
• raising social awareness	• companionship
• learning to count their blessings	• looking after babies and young children
• character building	• the challenge of helping

i) Raising social awareness

Foster carers put considerable emphasis on how fostering helped to raise their children's social awareness about child care need. They suggested the children became, as a result, more caring, more considerate and more understanding. Typical examples included:

Our children have learnt a lot about life for others. They have been able to care and help too, which can only be a benefit.

It has helped them understand about life's hardships.

Fostering, in the parents' view, also helped their children to broaden their thinking and 'open their eyes'. They 'learnt to care for others' or 'developed understanding about "special needs" children' or generally fostering 'made them more aware of other children's difficulties'.

A boy of 15 in Part's (1993) study is reported to have said on the same theme that he was:

. . . more socially aware than children who do not foster.

Pugh (1996) also reported on how some young people she spoke to displayed 'a striking concern for others and awareness of complex emotional issues beyond their years'. As one of them put it:

It makes me feel quite sad. Some of the things you hear are horrendous.

ii) Learning to count their blessings

For some carers, fostering made their children become aware of how more fortunate they were than other children. It was seen as 'good' for them to see others who were 'worse off' than themselves. This realisation, it was claimed, made their own children more 'appreciative' of what they had, such as a home, a family and parents:

Fostering has helped them understand about life's hardships and how lucky they are.

It is good for them to see others worse off than themselves.

Similarly, a 20-year-old lad in Part's (1993) study commented:

You realise how lucky you are to live in a caring family.

iii) Character building

Many carers attached considerable importance to certain values, learnt and developed through fostering, contributing overall to character building. They included learning to share and being more understanding and considerate. Such an experience was seen as helping to shape their children's character in the right direction. There were descriptions of how their children learnt to share their toys, their pets, friends and even parents, though sometimes they equally felt 'jealous' perceiving the foster child as a 'rival'. The following is a sample of typical comments:

More caring, more understanding, more sharing, more patient and kind.

It helps them with a sense of values and makes them less selfish.

The children were thought to develop greater altruism by becoming 'more tolerant' or 'less selfish'. A few parents also gave examples of how fostering helped their own children in a more direct and personal way such as 'to come out of their shyness', 'to adjust better', or 'become more confident'.

Looking at studies which interviewed children, the latter put more emphasis, than parents, on the benefits arising especially from companionship with some describing it as 'like having a younger brother or sister', 'someone to play with and read', 'making me laugh', 'always funny' or 'being able to help'(Part, 1993; Pugh, 1996).

b) Mixed or more negative reactions
Almost two-fifths (39 per cent) of carers who had own children living at home reported that their own children found the current foster child more difficult to get on with than they expected. Most of this entailed behavioural/emotional problems displayed by the foster children (54 per cent); this was followed by rivalry/jealousy (23 per cent); invasion of space (11 per cent) and sexualised behaviour (4 per cent). Also important were the kind of behaviours own children found 'disturbing' or 'annoying' which included verbal or physical attacks, withdrawal, moodiness, sleeping problems, destructiveness and/or stealing and lying. Parents in this group focused their explanations on four main areas: the foster child's behaviour problems; jealousy and rivalry; own children getting less attention; and having no privacy.

i) Behavioural/emotional
The kind of behaviours that own children found 'annoying', 'off-putting' or made them 'angry' included: 'taking their own belongings without permission', 'destructiveness of personal belongings', 'use of abusive language', 'screaming during the night', 'the calling of names' or displaying 'disruptive behaviour making own children angry and resentful'.

One carer added:
Our youngest child can't understand why we are doing it.

Other parents were particularly worried about the bad feelings and resentment some behaviours were raising in their own children, but more so when there were episodes of attack or the less frequent demonstration of sexualised behaviour on the part of the foster child. Some foster children were seen as 'more worldlywise' generating fears in carers that their own children might suffer or try to copy some of the behaviours. As one of many carers in this group put it:

Fostering can be very hard on your own children.

Some carers suggested that more careful matching should help minimise some of these fears and possibilities. However, there can be no risk-proof matching if carers are to work with more difficult children.

Considering that some of the problems that usually arise between own and foster children have to do with inconsistent handling, foster carers at times found themselves having to develop clear rules and expectations about the way things were to be done, and be consistent in their handling of all children. Notwithstanding this, own children would sometimes complain that the parents were 'making too many excuses for the foster child' or that foster children were allowed 'to get away with it'. Social workers too were sometimes perceived by own children as tolerating unacceptable behaviours in foster children and even offering them 'treats'. Some carers, in their effort to promote better understanding of the foster child's needs, found themselves uncertain of how much background information to share with their children without breaking confidentiality.

ii) Jealousy and rivalry

It was perhaps to be expected that a fair amount of the negative reactions of own children would focus on rivalries, jealousies and competition between them and the fostered children. This was more usual when the children were very young and of about the same age. One parent said: 'Too much jealousy; they rarely communicate'.

There were references to 'regular squabbles' and own children feeling 'left out' in sharing their parents. What worried these carers most was that their children sometimes came to feel as 'second best' to the foster child, that 'their needs were not as important', or that they had to share, for example, a father who was not often at home. A toddler placed with a single carer with a six-month-old baby was apparently so jealous of the attention paid to the baby that he would attack the baby with a knife. We also had a couple of examples where the carers were concerned about the aggressive behaviour of their own child towards the newcomer.

A minority of carers singled out bad feelings between the children which arose out of what they described as the 'lavish' way the Department was treating the foster child. Reference was made to expensive clothes, designer footwear, outings with the social worker and eating at expensive places. All this generated resentment in their own child. Interestingly, though, a broadly similar proportion of different carers criticised the social work services for not providing adequately for the foster child.

iii) Own children getting less attention
Unsurprisingly some of the foster children were very attention seeking, wanting to be the only child in the household or to monopolise the attention of the adult carers. Some carers held the view that very demanding children should be matched with either childless carers or those whose own children had grown up. Otherwise they felt that:

It was a high price to pay.

iv) Having no space or privacy
It was perhaps to be expected that some of the "host" children would come to feel that their "space" had been invaded or that they had no privacy left. Where the children got on well with each other, or where there was a big age gap and they kept out of each other's way, the problem seemed less pronounced. Otherwise, it was claimed by some carers that their children 'didn't feel at home in their own home'.

c) Sharing between own and foster children
Carers were also asked to rate how their children felt about sharing a number of people and things with the foster children. Their answers are set out in Table 9.3.

Table 9.3
How sharing were own children?*

Sharing	Always objected %	Usually objected %	Sometimes objected %	Hardly ever objected %	Never objected %	All %
Own room	8	3	27	20	42	100
Belongings	3	6	37	26	28	100
Friends	3	6	25	22	44	100
Father	3	8	26	20	43	100
Mother	3	6	35	20	36	100
Pets	4	3	15	21	57	100
Average	**4**	**5**	**28**	**22**	**41**	**100**

*This table excludes carers with no own children or whose children were no longer at home.

Taking all five areas, around one in ten children always or usually objected to sharing either things or their parents and friends; almost two-thirds either hardly ever or never objected to sharing; and the rest, around (28 per cent) sometimes objected. The greatest objection, though not statistically significant, was about sharing their belongings and their mother. On the whole, own children came across as sharing and considerate, largely confirming Part's (1993) and Pugh's (1996) findings on their enjoyment of fostering.

d) Proximity in age between own and foster children
Starting with Parker's (1966) study over 30 years ago, subsequent research in foster care has consistently identified a connection between placement breakdowns and close proximity in age between foster and own children (for a summary of studies see Triseliotis, 1989). Our data did not allow for testing this conclusion in terms of the proportion of breakdowns but we were able to do so in another way. We contrasted the number and proportion of own children who were said by their parents to have found the current foster child more difficult than expected, with the proximity in age and the sex of the placed child.

Of the 1,194 foster children featuring in the sample, 211 (or 18 per cent) were placed in 162 fostering households where one or more own children were of the same age or within one or two years of the foster child's age. Table 9.4 shows that half of these foster children were perceived to be more difficult than expected, which is considerably more than the figure for the whole sample. When only children of exactly the same age are considered, the proportion rises to 63 per cent, much more than the 39 per cent for the whole sample (Ch. sq: 0. 01). This risk held almost constant irrespective of the child's age at placement. Unlike other studies which looked at breakdowns, this only examined difficulties within continuing placements and it may explain why the relationship found within a one or two years' proximity was not as strong. A further analysis indicated that it did not also matter whether or not children were of the same or opposite sex.

Table 9.4

Proximity in age between foster and own children*

Age group of foster children and proximity in age	Own child found foster child difficult		Own child did not find foster child difficult		Total	
	N	%	N	%	N	%
Same age as own	37	63	22	37	59	36
One year difference	23	43	30	57	53	33
Two years difference	19	38	31	62	50	31
All	**79**		**83**		**162**	**100**

* *This table excludes carers with no own children or own children over 21.*

Based on her small scale study, Downes (1987) urged caution in making placements 'where children (own) are less than four years younger than fostered teenagers' because tensions mount as the age gap narrows and 'there is a tendency for such placements to be short and disrupt' (pp 14–15). During the analysis of the data, we were struck by the number of carers who said that they asked for a foster child who should not be older than any of their children, mainly to avoid the possible 'domination' of their own. To test this notion, the next table contrasts the experiences of own children in relation to foster children who were older than themselves by under or over five years and by all children placed.

Of the 153 households we had information about where older than own children were placed, 62 (or 41 per cent) of the fostered children were found by own children to be more difficult than expected. This is only slightly higher than the average of 39 per cent for all placements where there were underage own children. Problems, however, went up to 50 per cent when the difference in age was under five years and down to 28 per cent when the difference was five or more years. In other words, placing children in households where there are younger children by less than five years carries higher risks (Ch. sq: 0. 01). In contrast, when the difference is more than five years the risk is well below the average.

Table 9.5
Own children's experiences in relation to fostered children who were older than themselves by more or under five years and by all placements*

Age gap	Problems		No problems		All	
	N	%	N	%	N	%
Under 5 years	43	50	43	50	86	100
5 years & over	19	28	48	72	67	100
	62	41	91	59	153	100
All placements	**205**	**39**	**326**	**61**	**531**	**100**

* *This table excludes carers with no own children or no own children over 21.*

PLACEMENT ENDING

The reaction of carers and their children to foster children leaving is likely to depend on the length of the placement, the age of the children, and the depth of relationships and attachments developed. A sizeable group of carers in the study (around one in ten) said that their children experienced strong feelings of sadness and sometimes distress when the foster child(ren) left. Their comments on this permeated many key questions asked of them. Some carers described how they themselves felt 'bereft', 'distressed', as if there had been 'a death in the family', or ' being very sad for weeks'. Similar feelings were said to have been experienced by their own children. For these carers, 'parting with the children was the 'worst aspect of fostering', they could think of.

My life became empty as each of the children left.

We had some very distressing times.

Many of these carers perceived social work staff as having missed the impact of such loss, while others noted having been criticised for losing their 'professionalism' through over-attachment. As one of them put it:

You cannot stop your child from playing with the foster child because they will get attached to each other.

The sense of loss experienced by some carers and their children and, we can assume, by the foster children, has also been highlighted by others (Berridge and Cleaver, 1987). Besides the lack of recognition for the loss and grief involved for the whole fostering family, the frequent absence of feedback about how children are getting on only adds to the "weight" of grief. Some carers described the tears, sobbing and distress that their children went through, with some repeatedly asking when the foster child would be back. As one of them put it:

It was as if her world fell apart and I couldn't comfort her enough.

Strong attachments usually grew out of long-term placements, making separations even more difficult. Some of the criticism was particularly reserved for placements that were meant to last for a few weeks and instead went on for much longer periods. A handful of carers resented the removal of a child to go for adoption when they could have adopted the child themselves after caring for him/her for so long. Most carers recognised the "pain" arising out of seeing children leave as an inevitable part of fostering, but they found it difficult explaining it to their children and expected social workers to provide more recognition and support.

SUMMARY

- Many carers maintained that, if they became aware that their own children were in some way harmed by fostering, they would then terminate a specific placement or give up fostering altogether. From our sample of foster carers who had ceased to foster, we had a number of instances where this had actually happened.

- More encouragingly, the majority of carers indicated that the impact of fostering on their children was on the whole beneficial and helped develop many virtues and qualities in them, including social awareness and character formation. Own and foster children were reported to have a lot to offer to each other and it was not a one way process. Nevertheless, a significant minority of carers also said that fostering harmed their children in one way or another or made them feel less secure.

- It is important to refrain from placing children of the same age as that of an own child which has been found by this and other studies to carry significant risks. Similarly, avoid the placement of children who are older than the carers' own by less than five years.

10 Contact between children in foster care and their parents

BACKGROUND

Both policy and practice in Britain are now based on the assumption that, when children are fostered or in residential care, social workers and carers should strive to promote contact unless there is clear evidence that this is contrary to the child's welfare. The UN Convention on the Rights of the Child specifies that any child who is separated from one or both parents has the right 'to maintain personal relations and direct contact with both parents on a regular basis, except if it is contrary to the child's best interests' (Article 9).

UK child care legislation places considerable emphasis on the maintenance of links between looked after children and their families or others who have parental responsibility. Local authorities and foster carers are asked not just to enable contact to happen but to actively encourage and facilitate it. Parents too have a responsibility to keep in touch with their separated children.

In keeping with these principles, it is also expected that children's care plans and placement agreements will outline arrangements for contact with the child's family and other significant network members. With the support of their local authority, foster carers are seen as playing a pivotal role in encouraging a child or young person in their care to maintain family contact as set out in the care plan and also in supporting family members to do likewise.

Partnership has therefore become a catchword in current practice, but sharing the task of caring for children is not easy. Parents and foster carers each have a different kind of power and investment in the children's lives and often approach parenting with different attitudes and expectations. Commonly foster carers have children of their own, whose needs and interests have to be weighed alongside those of the children being looked after and their families. Values and child-rearing practices are likely to be different between families who have had to give up care of a child and those who have been approved to care for others' children. Tensions between carers and parents are thus to be expected and worked with rather than viewed as insurmountable problems.

In view of the emphasis placed by the legislation on contact and partnership, it is right to examine the empirical base, bearing in mind these contrasts in perspective between parents and foster carers.

THE EVIDENCE

First we review the evidence from previous research on the links between contact and three crucial dimensions of outcome:
- children's well-being and identity;
- their behaviours and adjustment; and
- early reunification.

Previous findings about processes of contact and foster carers' attitudes are also outlined.

Well-being and identity

Several studies have indicated that maintaining frequent contact with parents assists foster children's sense of belonging, identity, self-esteem and general well-being. Conversely, children with little or no contact generally have poorer outcomes. A seminal piece of American research was carried out by Weinstein (1960) on 'the self-image of the foster child'. In that study, Weinstein established that regular natural parent contact was statistically associated with the foster child achieving high scores on present and future "well-being" scales. At the same time, in Britain, Trasler (1960) also found that a lack of knowledge of what is happening to their families and themselves creates 'severe anxiety' in foster children, which is then reflected in their behaviour.

Some ten years later, in a study of adopted people, Triseliotis (1973) revealed how a positive identity and sense of self were closely linked to access to detailed genealogical and other background information, with opportunities for access to members of the original family. In a subsequent study of long-term foster care, Triseliotis (1980) concluded that 'knowledge by the child about his family of origin and the circumstances of his fostering contributes to feelings of well-being and to better adjustment' (p 157).

Millham *et al* (1986) found that many parents of children in foster and residential care felt unwanted and believed they had nothing more to contribute to the well-being of their children once they were away from home. Yet children themselves often yearn to see their parents and to have more information about their families. Of a sample of children living in foster homes, a third reported they would have liked to have seen more of their parents (Fletcher, 1993). From her small sample of children in long-term foster care, McAuley (1996) identified that, even after two years in placement, their feelings and thoughts were still strongly oriented to their birth parents, as well as friends and teachers from the past.

Behaviour and adjustment

Research has also found a connection between absence of contact and disturbance in children. One of these established that 57 per cent of foster children aged over one and a half years at placement with no parental contact were 'disturbed' as against only 35 per cent with regular contact (Jenkins, 1969). This observation was confirmed by Holman (1973) in a study of private fostering who also found that the less the contact the higher the incidence of certain emotional and physical symptoms such as soiling and ill-health. He also found that although regular visits were beneficial to the child, infrequent contact was associated with more fostering difficulties than no contact at all (Holman, 1980).

Thorpe (1974) reported that only 27 per cent of the children in her study had contact with their birth parents and less than half of these had contact as often as every three months. Her work again revealed a trend suggesting a relationship between satisfactory adjustment and contact, although it was not statistically significant except for 11 to 13-year-olds.

Reunification

Studies have consistently shown that one of the best predictors of reunification following reception into care is the maintenance of the links between the child and his/her family (Aldgate, 1980; Millham *et al*, 1986; Berridge and Cleaver, 1987). For example, Aldgate (1980) concluded that frequent contact between parents and children was an essential part of successful rehabilitation.

PROCESSES OF CONTACT

We have seen how most quantitative studies which have examined the frequency of contact between looked after children and their parents have found a strong correlation with favourable outcomes, including the likelihood of a relatively quick return home (Department of Health, 1991). Of course, some caution is needed in interpreting these repeated findings, since parents who are more caring and/or competent than others will tend to keep in touch and will usually also have children with less severe difficulties, so that good progress and a more rapid return home are only to be expected, compared with families where major and long-standing difficulties in parent–child relations occur. Thus it does not necessarily follow that increasing contact will invariably improve the child's prospects. However, research and practice have also shown that practical, attitudinal and institutional obstacles can interfere with the maintenance of helpful relationships between children and their families (Aldgate, 1980; Millham *et al*, 1986), so it is vital that such barriers to contact are minimised.

Among the factors which inhibit contact are:
- "filial deprivation", i.e. parents' sense of failure, loss and guilt which sap their motivation to keep in touch (Jenkins and Norman, 1972);
- practical difficulties such as distance and the cost of travel (Millham *et al*, 1986);
- restrictions placed by authorities (Bullock *et al*, 1993);
- mutual disenchantment and the absence of effective mediation for parents and older children (Fletcher, 1993; Triseliotis *et al*, 1995b);
- lack of commitment and support from social workers (Rowe *et al*, 1984; Kufeldt *et al*, 1989; Atherton, 1993);
- attitudes of carers, ranging from hostility to an absence of welcome or lack of understanding of parents' perspective (Aldgate, 1980; Millham *et al*, 1986);
- parental behaviour, e.g. drunkenness, aggression (Cleaver, 1997).

Triseliotis *et al* (1995a) set out a number of factors that have been found by research to contribute to increased contact. They include parents believing contact is valuable; a positive attitude by carers; early and consistent social work encouragement; and proximity between placement and parental home.

Carers' attitude to contact

A number of studies over the years have indicated that significant proportions of foster carers are ambivalent or even hostile towards parents. Longer placements, which usually reflect deep-rooted family problems, may exacerbate negativity. Wilkinson (1988) observed that 'as the placement period grew, foster parents tended to be openly critical and often hostile to the child's family' (p 236). Conversely, Reed (1993) reported that foster carers of children with learning disabilities were noticeably less positive about contact if they thought the child or young person might return home. In different ways, these findings indicate that, with time, there is a growing sense of possession of the foster child.

Holman (1980) distinguished between foster families with an 'exclusive' orientation, who mainly wanted to integrate the child into their own family with minimal involvement of the birth family, and families who were 'inclusive' in approach. He wrote:

The inclusive concept of fostering favours continued contact with natural parents and imparting background knowledge to the children. Exclusive fostering tends towards the opposite (p 78).

He cited earlier research indicating that inclusive fostering tended to be more successful. McAuley (1996) reported that those children in her sample who did not feel they had permission from their foster carers for contact felt 'sad and angry' (p 115).

Given the general trend towards greater professionalisation of foster carers' roles, the development of specialist schemes and changing policy emphases, it might be expected that present-day carers will be much more inclusive than in the past, as appears to be the case in residential care (Berridge and Brodie, 1998). On the other hand, nowadays many looked after children have parents whose past or current actions may tax the most flexible of carers. These include violence, substance misuse and child abuse (Cleaver, 1997). Our own study provided evidence about the present position.

THE PRESENT STUDY

Among other things, the present study asked carers to answer a number of questions on contact including work with the children's parents, general and more specific attitudes towards parents, views on contact, benefits for children from seeing their parents, where the children met their parents, difficulties with visits, and contact within the foster home.

Attitudes to parents

Carers were asked specific questions on this topic. In addition, some carers spontaneously referred to parents in response to more general questions about their experience of fostering. Both types of information are included here, beginning with the more general comments.

General attitudes towards parents

In terms of their motivation to foster, few carers mentioned wanting to work with parents. Mostly they referred to their fondness and concern for children and a desire to help. In response to various open-ended questions about their experience of fostering, carers referred much more frequently to children and social workers than to parents. When parents were mentioned, comments were more often negative than supportive.

Only 15 carers (two per cent) cited working with parents as an aspect of fostering they enjoyed, while around eight per cent named this as one of the worst elements of their role. Nearly one in ten carers said that parents' attitudes and behaviour sometimes made them feel like stopping fostering. About 12 per cent of carers gave at least one negative response about parents, while only 15 carers (two per cent) made spontaneous positive comments about working with parents.

From both the questionnaires and the interviews, it seemed that many did not fully understand what was expected of them with regard to "working with parents". The same uncertainty and lack of detail were also found in many of the local authority guidelines on foster care. One in ten carers felt unprepared for "dealing" with parents, though only a handful of these expressed a wish for more training in this aspect. Few carers expressed concerns about how best to work with parents, but more often voiced censure of parents' behaviour or fears of an allegation against them or a member of their family. Understandably, carers tended to be especially critical when parents had abused children in their care. It is worth noting an innovative recent initiative involving birth parents in the ongoing training of foster carers as a way of easing and improving relations between foster carers and birth parents (Gilchrist and Hoggan, 1996).

The frequency of carers' comments on how sad they felt when children left also highlighted how emotionally difficult it is for adults to share children's care. When asked what prevented people from fostering, carers cited children returning home as a common drawback and children leaving was viewed as the fourth worst aspect of fostering. Some carers had felt ill-prepared for the emotional impact of fostering and wanted more recognition of how difficult it is to manage the feelings generated by parting with children. Equally disturbing and off-putting for some of them was seeing children getting upset following contact and when let down by parents.

Carers' attitudes to current foster children's parents

We asked carers to rate both how easy it was to get on with the children's parents and how appreciated the parents made them feel. Perhaps surprisingly, given the tensions mentioned above, the majority of carers indicated that they and the children's parents got on reasonably well (Table 10.1). Approximately half said they always or mostly found it easy to get on with the parents while one in six said it was rarely or never easy to relate to them.

Table 10.1
Relating to children's parents

	N	%
Easy all the time	106	16
Mostly easy	232	35
Sometimes easy and sometimes difficult	207	32
Rarely easy	45	7
Never easy	68	10
Total	***658**	**100**

*125 (15 per cent) of carers indicated they had no contact with the birth parents and a further 39 did not answer this question.

Those who found the parents seldom or never easy were invited to explain why these relationships were difficult. Their responses mostly reflected the tensions of working in partnership when the child is in care against the parents' wishes:

> *They resent the fact that you have their child.*

> *Parents try to wind children up against the carers.*

> *They see us as the enemy.*

When it came to rating the extent to which carers felt valued or appreciated by parents, approximately 40 per cent felt appreciated, a quarter did not feel appreciated, and just under a third (31 per cent) gave the middle rating. In contrast, two-thirds felt appreciated or very appreciated by the children and only eight per cent felt the opposite.

Thus although there was little evidence of sustained work undertaken by foster carers with parents, most relationships with individual parents were reported to be reasonably good. There was little scope within the survey to assess the quality of these relationships further or explore how they contributed to plans for children. However, we did ask about attitudes and practice in relation to children's contact with their parents, recognising that the contact visit can be an important means for foster carers to get to know and demonstrate their "partnership" with parents.

Views on contact

Before obtaining information about arrangements for current foster children to meet with their parents, we posed three general questions about carers' views on contact:

- Do you see benefits from children seeing their parents?
- How helpful is it to have social workers present during visits?
- Where do you prefer foster children to see their parents?

Benefits from children seeing parents

Almost two-thirds of carers said they did recognise benefits from children seeing their parents while only eight per cent did not. Just under a third gave a qualified answer, saying that they were unsure and that it depended on the circumstances. A higher proportion of carers who received a fee, in addition to the fostering allowance, recognised that there were benefits for children seeing their parents. A typical positive response was:

> *The children need to know who their parents are and keep in touch, especially if they are going to return home.*

In all, over a third of carers were less enthusiastic about contact with parents. While a number stressed that it depended on the individual situation, others expressed a range of mixed feelings about the value of contact in general. Typical comments included:

> *I'm not very convinced, especially in the case of children who have been abused. Any visits should be supervised. In the majority, contact does not help the children.*

> *Contacts were seen as important for the children but I had doubts about the last one. Could see no benefit.*

> *I'm not convinced unless there is a good relationship between the child and the parents. I might allow a young mother to come to teach her how to feed and bathe a baby but not an abuser.*

Sometimes it was explained that contact was undesirable or should be reduced because children were upset or could still be at risk from abusive parents. Others saw contact as benefiting parents rather than children:

I think it is of greater value to the parents than to the children.

Even some of those who were committed to promoting contact in principle nevertheless had encountered situations in which they doubted whether it was in the best interests of the children. For instance, one said:

I would bend over backwards to promote contact or take children to their homes but am not convinced about its value for all children.

From these and similar comments it seemed that a substantial minority of foster carers thought that social work policy and practice over-emphasised the value of contact in a way which was not always in the child's interests.

Preferred meeting place between parents and children

When it came to where parents and children should meet, of 674 who expressed a clear preference, two out of five preferred meetings to take place in the parental home, just under a third preferred the foster home, and another third preferred social work offices or family centres. Reflecting the tensions which arise when children are cared for by another family, especially if against the wishes of the parents, there were also some suggestions that visits should take place on neutral ground, where parents and children could relax. Such observations were reminiscent of what research and practice have told us about contact between separated or divorced parents and their children.

Some carers readily valued the idea of parents visiting the foster home. One person summed up a number of potential advantages:

It is important that the parent comes to see the children where they live, and that they are safe, where they sleep, their toys. As a carer you also need acceptance and approval from the parent. I know what vital parts parents play. They also make the job so much easier.

At the opposite end of the spectrum, some carers were not prepared to have access within their home at all:

It has to be away from our home as we prefer to keep it that way and no intrusion in our family.

Would prefer all visits to be away from us.

Social worker picks up child and takes to parents.

Negative comments about visits within the foster home may simply indicate that carers felt under pressure, but in some instances they seemed to be indicative of a lack of sympathy for the parents, an attitude which could create difficulties for children who may find themselves having to bridge an uncomfortable gap between the important adults in their lives.

Current arrangements for contact

Foster carers were also asked a number of questions about contact between the children they were currently looking after and their parents. Of course children may meet other members of their family but, in the interests of brevity, we asked only about contact with parents. We firstly asked where the children met with their parents. Some carers referred to more than one location, presumably indicating that there were different arrangements for different children or that arrangements differed for the same child. Excluding the 130 (15 per cent) whose foster children had no contact at all with parents, the locations for contact were as shown in Figure 10.1.

Figure 10.1
Where children saw their parents

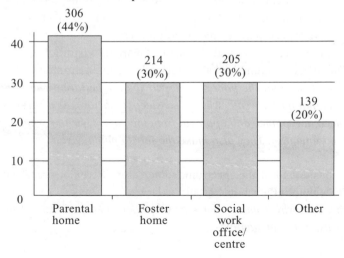

When this information was compared with carers' preferences about where children and their parents should meet, it was evident that, at least in terms of location, actual arrangements closely reflected carers' wishes. Furthermore, only 15 per cent said they would have wanted visits to take place somewhere else. Almost a third of them expressed considerable support for a comfortably furnished room in a relaxed and neutral setting.

Difficulties with contact visits

Just over half (55 per cent) of the carers whose foster children were in contact with parents said they had experienced difficulties over these contact visits. The proportion was the same whether visits took place within the foster home or elsewhere. Some of the difficulties related to events in the past which influenced carers' current willingness to welcome parents into their home. One carer summed this up as follows:

> Been attacked once by natural parent. After that, no more access for anyone in my home.

Evidently, exposure to violence makes the cosy notion of partnership especially difficult to achieve and requires careful planning and support from social workers. In order of frequency the problems cited were as shown in Table 10.2 below.

Table 10.2
Problems experienced with contact visits

	Contact elsewhere		Contact in foster home	
	N	%	N	%
Parents not turning up or otherwise letting children down	118	23	49	23
Parents' behaviour	96	19	46	21
Child upset after contact	66	13	8	4
Disruption to the foster family	46	9	28	13

Descriptions of problems referred to the impact on the child and the foster family. Typical comments included:

Children regress after visits.

Parents let children down by not turning up or being drunk.

Parents can be aggressive and incite unsuitable behaviour in the children.

Other difficulties resulted from differences in values, for instance, parents not liking how the children were dressed, 'turning the child to bad habits' or not keeping to agreed times. Complaints also concerned parents described as disrupting foster family routines by staying too long in the foster home, coming at unscheduled hours or being late. This highlights the difficulties which can arise in carrying out professional tasks while functioning as an ordinary family. Presumably carers can only be expected to cope with this level of disruption if they are well supported and are paid appropriately (Triseliotis *et al*, 1998). Nevertheless, only a small proportion (six per cent) of those who said that fostering did not meet with their expectations cited 'parental interference' as the main reason.

Contact within the foster home
Of those carers who indicated that at least one of their foster children was in touch with his or her parents, just under a third were hosting contact visits within their own home. These meetings can be an important means through which foster carers come to understand the child's family situation, offer support to parents, and help the child cope with belonging to two families. Likewise these give birth parents more detailed understanding of the foster home and symbolise for the children that the significant adults in their lives are spending time together and co-operating. At the same time our respondents indicated that having parents visit the home could be stressful and disruptive and may deter people from fostering. Kufeldt *et al* (1989) observed that it is vital for social workers to be actively involved with visiting arrangements in order to support the child and carers, and to assess interaction.

Given the potential importance of home contact, we tried to identify more clearly those factors which might influence whether children saw their parents within their foster home or not. Factors relating to agency, placement, child, natural parent and foster family were considered.

Agency variations and contact

The proportion of carers having contact visits in their own home ranged from 16 to 50 per cent depending on the authority. One possible explanation may be the distance between the carers' and the children's parents' homes. There may also be differences in policy or accepted practice.

Table 10.3 sets out the proportion of foster carers currently having contact at their home for different types of placement. With the exception of community caring (specialist schemes for older children), the type of placement did not appear to make a marked difference to whether or not the parents visited their home. While the average was around 30 per cent, only 15 per cent who offered community caring had parents visiting their home. Probably the reason for this is that older children may prefer to see their parents elsewhere and are more able to travel independently to go home. Indeed some carers said they preferred to foster older children as it usually involves little family contact. In interviews we were told that most teenagers tended to make their own arrangements for contact, mostly away from the foster home. In some cases, the foster carers had not met the parents or perhaps only at the start of the care experience.

Table 10.3
Contact in the foster home by type of placement

Pre adoption	45%
Mixture	38%
Short term	32%
Emergency	32%
Respite	26%
Medium term/temporary	28%
Long term	23%
Community carers	15%

Child-related factors and contact

The level of perceived difficulty of the current foster children did not appear to be critical to whether or not children met their parents at the foster home. Of the families who indicated that at least one current foster child was more difficult than they had expected, 28 per cent had visits at their home. Where the child was not seen as difficult, the proportion was 34 per cent.

However, age and gender of foster children seemed to have some influence on whether the foster home would be the location for visits. Carers who looked after younger children and girls were somewhat more likely to have parents visit their home. Until age 10–13, gender differences were quite marked. Foster carers caring for girls were more likely to have contact visits at their homes than those with boys.

Parent-related factors and contact

As might be expected, there were more visits within the foster home if the carer(s) found it easy to get on with the parents. Among those who always or mostly found it easy to get on with parents, 36 per cent had contact visits in the foster home, compared with 33 per cent when the relationship was mixed and 20 per cent when carers rarely or never found the parents easy. Similarly, carers who thought that parents appreciated their work with the child and who acknowledged the value of contact were somewhat more likely to have parents visit their home.

Carer-related factors and contact

Although we have indicated that the practice of having contact visits in the foster home varied to some extent across authorities and in relation to some child and parent-related factors, in none of these instances did the association reach statistical significance. It was only in relation to carers that a statistically significant association was identified. Interestingly a higher proportion of foster carers who had been fostering for over 10 years had contact visits within their home, compared with those who began in the last 10 years. Correspondingly, carers who had fostered more than ten children were also significantly more likely to have contact within their home. This could indicate that recently approved carers may be less willing to have contact at home, that social workers' expectations of foster carers in this respect are changing, or that managing contact within the home is a difficult task which only the more experienced carers feel confident enough to tackle.

Responding to our findings, a number of foster care managers acknowledged that, in order to recruit or to ease pressures on existing foster carers, expectations in relation to hosting contact within the foster home would sometimes be reduced.

Social workers being present during contact visits

Views differed on how helpful it was to have social workers present during contact visits, with a number of carers stressing that it depended on the situation and age of the child. Almost a fifth said that the presence of the social worker was 'not usually helpful'. In spite of the mixed views about the presence of social workers, there was widespread agreement that if social workers were present their main role would be to help deal with difficult or aggressive parents. Foster carers especially singled out aggressive and "violent" parents or parents who were on drugs or arrived drunk. Typical comments on when social workers could help included:

When the parents are aggressive or try to take the children away or are on drugs.

When a parent is emotional, aggressive or out to cause trouble, i.e. allegations.

During disputes between parents and foster carers.

There was also support for a social work presence when parents had been abusive in the past, especially where a child had been sexually abused. Some foster carers felt they were expected to take on too much responsibility for visits, coping with the practical as well as emotional dimensions.

The social worker should collect the children and have somewhere to take them to meet parents. Too often this is left to the foster carers. Now you have to open your door to all sorts and be verbally abused sometimes.

The demands on carers were multiplied when they had to arrange visits for children from more than one family or from separated parents.

One carer commented that contact visits provided an opportunity for social workers to witness at first hand child–parent interaction but nobody identified a more pro-active role for them, like helping to develop the relationship between parent, foster carer or children. The main role seen for social workers was to help contain situations or protect carers, not to act as possible mediators and promote relationships. There was a clear message that carers often felt vulnerable during visits in their home.

SUMMARY

- Almost all previous studies have identified the positive contribution of parental contact to the children's well-being and reunification. The great majority of carers in our survey found fostering hard and demanding, but also rewarding. Many of them also felt overloaded by difficult children and increased demands. Contact was one more demand made on the carers, their time and sometimes their privacy and their family life. While the majority of foster carers were well disposed towards parents and recognised the importance of continuing contact, negative attitudes were also quite common. These mainly related to concerns about a) perceived negative impact on the child and b) disruption, conflict or aggression affecting the fostering household.
- The present arrangements for contact between children and their parents were broadly in line with foster carers' preferences and only a minority of children saw their parents at the foster home. This means that most foster children experienced little informal contact between their parents and carers.
- Some carers indicated they had felt ill-prepared for working with parents and for anticipating the emotional stress of caring for other people's children. They said they would like more ongoing support to cope with the powerful feelings generated by fostering.
- Carers who had been fostering for more than ten years were significantly more likely to have contact visits in their own homes than those who had started fostering more recently. While pay, training and

support may increase foster carers' willingness and readiness to encourage contact, concerns about intrusion into their homes is likely to persist, especially as many have children of their own to consider.

- Birth parents were sometimes blamed for their children's hardship which may make it difficult to include them in the restorative process. In addition, and leaving aside of what is meant by 'working with parents', caring for the children seemed to leave many carers with little time or energy to work with parents.
- Contact featured in the preparatory sessions but was not usually part of continuing training to reinforce its importance. Terms such as asking carers to "work with parents" were also found to lack meaning and detail of how this is to be done.

11 The delivery of fostering services

This chapter is in two parts. After introducing the main fostering tasks, part I reports the carers' levels of satisfaction with the delivery of the fostering services. Part II focuses on the agencies' response and perspective on the role and tasks of children's social workers and placement (link) workers who are responsible for the delivery of the service.

THE FOSTERING SERVICE

The introductory chapter made reference to a number of studies which attributed the local authorities' failure to retain carers, and/or the high levels of foster care breakdowns, to slow or no response to the carers' requests over difficulties with the children, carers feeling undervalued and unsupported, and children staying too long without an allocated social worker (Sellick, 1992; Bebbington and Miles, 1990; Caesar *et al*, 1994; Berridge, 1997; Butler and Charles, 1999).

The delivery of fostering services within the Scottish authorities was mainly in the hands of two types of workers and their first line managers: Children's Social Workers (CSW) and Placement (link) workers. The main fostering tasks could be summarised into the following three overlapping activities: recruiting, preparing, assessing and training carers; assessing and making decisions about the child, including matching children to carers; and an ongoing service provided to the children, the foster carers and the birth family.

Placement (link) workers and children's social workers
The introduction of the placement worker to the fostering service dates from about 1980 onwards. Before that, the roles of social worker and placement worker were mostly combined into one. At present, only in a handful of authorities do the two roles continue to be held by a single worker. With few exceptions, all carers now have a placement worker allocated to them.

The expectation of authorities is that they will define the general role of children's social workers and placement workers, while more specific requirements will feature in the individual agreements drawn up in relation to each child, parent and carer. It was more likely for authorities to define in writing the role of the placement worker than that of the child's social worker.

Placement workers, mostly attached to placement units, were seen by their managers as having specialist knowledge and expertise in fostering placement work. Their work was often combined with adoption, day care, respite work and occasionally throughcare. A key role for them was foster home finding, assessing new carers, matching children and carers and providing training and general support to carers. Several service managers also looked upon the placement worker as "mediators" in possible disputes between children's social workers and carers.

Social workers attached to child care area teams assessed children for placement, offered ongoing face-to-face services to children in foster care and to their families, and acted as support workers to carers in relation to the placed child. Besides this, they also carried responsibilities which included child protection work, case management, assessment and welfare-based support to families.

Agency manuals usually defined the role of the social worker in relation to the children in general terms. For example, 'all children and young people in a foster placement will be allocated a qualified worker' or a qualified worker will be appointed to 'support and assist children'. Only a couple of manuals made more explicit reference to 'direct work' or 'communication with children'. In other words, what was mostly missing was guidance on the nature of the professional task with children. Most of the emphasis, instead, was placed on procedural and indirect forms of work, including providing support to parents and carers. Some managers observed, though, that they intended to use the placement agreement to allocate more specific tasks and responsibilities.

Our discussions also led us to the conclusion that, in spite of the responsibility shared between children's social workers and placement workers to deliver the fostering service, not infrequently the fostering service came to be identified with its placement part to the exclusion of the important work undertaken by the child's social worker.

PART I

THE CARERS' VIEWS ON THE DELIVERY OF THE SERVICE

This section describes the carers' views of their working relationships and experiences with the child's social worker, their placement worker, and with the department/agency as a whole. The great majority of carers favoured the division of responsibility between children's social workers and placement workers. Questions were asked in relation to the child currently fostered and covered working relationships; frequency of visiting; interests; being available when needed; and appreciation.

The children's social workers

Carers were asked to rate the above five dimensions of contact with the current or most recent child's social worker. Table 11.1 shows that carers rated general relationships, interest and appreciation on the part of the social worker as good or very good, but they were less positive about frequency of visits and availability. Three out of ten carers found the latter 'poor', 'very poor' or as 'neither good nor poor'. Relatively few carers described the frequency of visits and availability as 'very good'. Much of the carers' dissatisfaction with the child's social worker had to do with:

- infrequent visits and unavailability;
- failing to provide sustained work with the children;
- failure to provide sufficient information on the children's background; and
- poor overall support.

What the carers were saying in their comments was that the children especially, and then themselves, were not receiving the support and direct input that was necessary and/or promised. Based on their findings, the authors of a recent study stressed the importance of direct work with children and young people as likely to prevent placement breakdown (Butler and Charles, 1999).

Table 11.1

Quality of interactions between carer and the child's social worker on five dimensions

Level	General relations N	%	Visits frequency N	%	Interest N	%	Availability N	%	Appreciation N	%
Very good	373	46	169	21	272	34	201	26	276	35
Good	254	32	383	49	378	48	349	44	353	45
Neither good nor bad	106	13	67	8	63	8	89	11	121	16
Poor	48	6	123	16	45	6	108	14	14	2
Very poor	25	3	44	6	29	4	37	5	14	2
Total	**806**	**100**	**786**	**100**	**787**	**100**	**784**	**100**	**778**	**100**

More of the carers who were unhappy about the availability of the social worker and/or frequency of visits also:
- found the children more difficult than expected;
- found that their expectations of fostering were not met;
- thought about giving up fostering;
- needed a break/respite; and
- said that the department could do more for its carers.

In contrast, those fostering for a special scheme and/or receiving a fee (mostly the same carers) were more likely than others to describe their relationship with the social workers as 'very good' than 'good', describe visits as sufficiently frequent, and to have felt understood.

As with other aspects of practice, carers held the view that there were again variations between authorities of both the frequency of visits and availability of social workers. For example, in one authority, over 80 per cent of carers described the frequency of visits as 'very good' to 'good' compared to 56 per cent in another large authority. Availability was rated at 88 per cent at the 'very good' and 'good' levels in one authority but only 60 per cent in some others. Somewhat smaller differences were noted with appreciation, interest and relationships. (Because the themes of visits, availability, valuing and appreciation appear in different contexts, these will be discussed in greater detail in the chapter on support.)

The placement worker

Placement workers were rated on the same five dimensions as social workers (see Table 11.2). In all, 90 per cent of carers who had a placement worker rated the relationship with their placement worker as 'very good' or 'good'. Only two per cent rated it as 'poor' or 'very poor'. In fact, almost seven out of ten rated their relationship with the link worker as having been 'very good' which was significantly higher compared to that accorded to the children's social workers. Levels of satisfaction were not as high in the other dimensions, but they were again significantly higher than those accorded to children's social workers. Only a few carers expressed dissatisfaction concerning interest or appreciation but there was some dissatisfaction with frequency of visits and availability; almost all those dissatisfied with the frequency of visits and availability of their placement workers were from predominantly rural authorities. Geographical considerations may explain some, but not all, the differences.

Table 11.2

Quality of interactions between carer and placement/link workers on five dimensions

Level	General relations		Visits frequency		Interest		Availability		Appreciation	
	N	%	N	%	N	%	N	%	N	%
V. good	479	68	291	45	350	53	314	48	312	48
Good	157	22	289	45	250	38	266	42	257	40
50/50	55	8	35	5	46	7	40	6	66	10
Poor	9	1	23	4	6	1	28	4	5	1
V. poor	10	1	9	1	6	1	8	1	4	1
Total	**710**	**100**	**647**	**100**	**659**	**100**	**656**	**100**	**644**	**100**

Levels of persistent satisfaction/dissatisfaction

We toyed for some time with the idea of developing an overarching composite picture of satisfaction based on the five attributes that featured in the previous tables. The main danger of doing this is that it detracts from the uniqueness of each individual component, such as availability, listening or appreciation. For example, the importance of a single component, such as availability which was central to carers' concerns, could easily be submerged within an overall level of performance. Nevertheless, it was decided to do this to provide a more generalised picture of satisfaction and dissatisfaction and to establish what proportion of carers were consistently satisfied or dissatisfied with most or all of these attributes with each type of worker.

Based on these calculations, the next figure shows that almost seven out of ten carers were consistently 'very satisfied' or 'satisfied' with their children's social workers on four or more of the five attributes, that is, quality of relationships, frequency of visits, availability, interest and appreciation. On the same basis, some 16 per cent were consistently 'dissatisfied' or 'very dissatisfied' and another 16 per cent 'mildly' dissatisfied, that is, usually dissatisfied with one attribute. As seen from Table 11.1, though, dissatisfaction with individual attributes such as frequency of visits and availability was higher than this overall level.

In contrast to the overall picture presented on children's social workers, 88 per cent of carers were consistently 'satisfied' or 'very satisfied' with their placement workers and six per cent were 'dissatisfied' or 'very dissatisfied'. Around five per cent of carers were dissatisfied with both.

The higher levels of satisfaction with link workers, compared to social workers, were mainly related to their:
- being more available and responsive;
- having more in depth understanding of fostering issues;
- continuity in the same post; and
- giving their undivided attention to carers.

The lower levels of satisfaction expressed by carers in relation to children's social workers, compared to link workers, and their accounts of the limitations of support services provided to them and the children

Figure 11.1

Levels of consistent satisfaction/dissatisfaction with social workers and placement workers

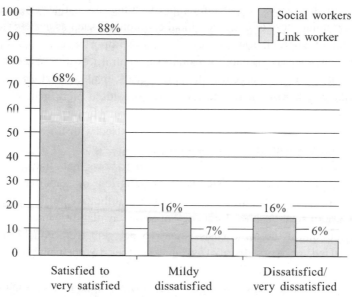

was one of the main gaps in service provision found by the study. Though we had many positive and enthusiastic comments about many children's social workers, those for placement workers were far in excess. The following is a typical comment on placement workers:

She was a gem. She had great communication skills and made you feel relaxed. If there was a problem, she would be the first one to get in touch. She was also very good at returning messages, was aware of what was going on and was very supportive.

Foster carer satisfaction and organisational structures

The introductory chapter highlighted the debate over whether the way the fostering service is organised makes any difference to carer satisfaction and to the outcomes for children. However, as shown in Chapter 2, the similarity in the way the fostering services were organised do not allow for too many contrasts to be made. In spite of these limitations, a couple of tentative conclusions were drawn based on the carers' level of satisfaction in relation to the activities of the placement worker.

Firstly, the ratings presented in Table 11.3 contrast carer satisfaction with placement workers based in units with the ratings provided for those based in area teams. Placement workers based in units were rated significantly higher, at the 'very good' level, on the *frequency of* visits and on *availability*, compared to placement staff based in area teams (Mantel-Haenzel .002). Authorities with units were, as a whole, also rated higher on the provision of overall support (Mantel-Haenzel .025) (see Table 11.3).

Secondly, taking the five attributes together, that is, frequency of visits, availability, interest, appreciation and quality of relationships, carers supported by link workers based in units were more likely to feel 'very satisfied' than simply 'satisfied' with them compared to the two authorities where the placement workers were attached to area teams. The geographical features, however, of the two authorities with area team attachments seem to have contributed to the lower levels of satisfaction, but the differences could not all be attributed to them. Not all of the authorities with centralised units gained approval, so evidently having a unit-based service by itself does not guarantee more satisfied carers.

Table 11.3

Contrasting levels of carer satisfaction between placement workers based in units and those attached to area teams with regard to frequency of visits, availability and support

Level	*Frequency of visits*		*Availability*		*Overall support*	
	Unit	*Area*	*Unit*	*Area*	*Unit*	*Area*
	%	%	%	%	%	%
Very good	48	28	49	34	39	26
Good	42	46	41	42	36	36
Mixed	5	11	5	10	17	25
Poor or v. poor	5	15	4	14	8	13
Total %	**100**	**100**	**100**	**100**	**100**	**100**

The carers and the department as a whole

Carers were aware that many plans and decisions about individual children were made between the child's social worker and higher management, sometimes involving the directorate. They were equally aware that, when it came to additional resources and their distribution, higher management and elected representatives played the most decisive role. While being unclear about the exact processes involved in both cases, they mostly felt left out and peripheral. As a result they were less certain about their role and relationship with higher management, except that junior social workers were meant to be present at reviews.

The study asked carers to appraise the overall performance of the agency in relation to the operation of its fostering service. Leaving aside financial issues, which are discussed later in this chapter, three dimensions were selected concerning the operation of the fostering service and the agency: overall level of support, quality of relationships, and appreciation by the management and agency as a whole.

Table 11.4

The carers' rating of support made available, quality of relationships and appreciation by the agency as a whole

	Support		Relationships		Appreciation	
Level	*N*	*%*	*N*	*%*	*N*	*%*
Very Good	292	37	295	37	213	28
Good	280	35	360	45	356	48
Neither good nor poor	143	18	101	13	133	18
Poor	53	7	31	4	29	4
Very poor	24	3	10	1	14	1
Total	**792**	**100**	**797**	**100**	**745**	**100**

The highest rating was accorded to authorities for quality of relationships and this was fairly consistent across authorities.

When it came to appreciation by the agency, only 28 per cent rated it as 'very good' compared to 48 per cent for link workers and 35 per cent for social workers. At the other end, only five per cent of carers described it as 'poor' or 'very poor', with another 18 per cent describing it as neither good nor poor. Outright dissatisfaction in some authorities was as low as three or four per cent, while in some others it was around 15 per cent. The age group 31–40 were least satisfied with relationships and also felt least appreciated by the agency. Those feeling less appreciated were more likely to think of giving up, to find the children more difficult than expected, and to feel that the agency could do more for its carers.

The concept of support dominated most of the qualitative replies to the questionnaire and it also featured largely in the personal interviews. An attempt was made to aggregate it by asking about the overall level of support provided by the most recent social worker(s) and the agency as a whole. Over seven out of ten carers described the level of support either as 'very good' or 'good', with 37 per cent describing it as 'very good'. One in ten described it as 'poor' or 'very poor', and another 18 per cent as 'half and half'. The least satisfied group was again those aged 31–40 and the most satisfied the over 50s. The more qualified the carers, the more critical they were of the support they had received. Those who were critical of the levels of support were also likely to:

- find the children more difficult;
- need respite;
- say that their expectations had not been met; and
- think 'often' or 'very often' of giving up fostering.

(The concept of 'support' is discussed at greater length in Chapter 13.)

Those fostering for community care schemes, and/or who were drawing a fee, were again more likely than the rest to give significantly higher ratings in the 'very good' grade than simply 'good'.

Teaching social workers

We present here answers to an open-ended question of what three things carers would like to teach social workers, as distinct from placement workers. The fact that three-quarters of the carers, including many of those who felt satisfied with the operation of the fostering services, took the opportunity to make suggestions illustrates their wish to see further improvements in the fostering service. As if confirming their previous comments and observations, most carers wanted to teach children's social workers (in order or importance) how to:

- be more available, more supportive and reliable;
- be better listeners;
- work more in partnership;
- understand what hard work fostering is;
- provide honest information about the children and their background;
- use more common sense;
- think of the carers' family;
- learn more about children; and
- sometimes act as foster carers.

How authorities as a whole could do more

When asked how authorities as a whole could do more, almost six out of ten carers made important suggestions and identified the following areas, in order of importance, as requiring attention:

- greater availability/support from social workers;
- to be listened to and valued more;
- better pay and conditions;
- more information and involvement, more of a partnership;
- more training;
- more respite.

PART II

THE AUTHORITIES' PERSPECTIVE ON SERVICE DELIVERY

The gaps in service delivery identified by carers led the study to seek information and ask questions of managers on aspects of service delivery, and especially about the specific roles of children's social workers and of placement workers.

Number of employed staff and workloads

We were especially keen to establish the proportion of part-time staff used, in view of a number of carers' criticisms about discontinuity of support to the children and themselves, but such information was not available.

The supposition is often made that different workloads carried by staff may also account for differences in performance. Though the work of social workers could be more easily measured in terms of individual cases carried, that of placement workers was more difficult. Besides offering support to individual carers, the latter also had responsibilities in relation to recruitment, assessment, the preparation and continued training of carers, and in matching. On the other hand, a social worker case is likely to be much more complex than the offer of support to individual carers. This is in addition to emergency work connected with child abuse investigations and assessments.

Placement workers 'looked after' an average of 17 foster carers each in contrast to 24 children's cases carried by children's social workers. (Almost two-fifths of authorities could not provide figures on social workers and a fifth on placement workers.) In our study there were wide variations between authorities in the number of cases carried. The highest average or single workload for social workers was 41 in one agency and the lowest 10 in another. The number of carers supported by individual placement workers ranged from eight to 26. The NFCA study in England found that placement workers carried a "median" of 19 carer units each (Waterhouse, 1997). The Audit Commission (1994) recommended that link workers should not have to support more than 20 foster households. Workloads were not found to be related to levels of carer satisfaction or to levels of recruitment.

Managers were unhappy with the workloads carried by both types of worker but far more so with those of the children's social workers. Typical comments made about the demands made on social workers' time included: 'too high caseloads' or 'unacceptably heavy'.

Frequency of visits to children by social workers

Because of many carers' criticisms about infrequent visits by social workers to themselves and the children, the questionnaire asked authorities to outline the frequency of visits and responses are set out in Table 11.5. The most common answer to the question was that visit frequency was 'variable' or 'depended on need'. Good social work practice would advise that frequency of visits should be agreed and specified within the placement agreement or within the care plan to reflect the needs of the case and also take account of unpredictabilities such as crises.

Table 11.5

Frequency of visits by social workers to children in foster care*

Every 2 weeks	3–4 weeks	Variable	Other	Total
%	%	%	%	%
24	8	60	8	100

Ɵ ɯ ɯ ɯɯ authorities did not answer this question. It is probable that some of the Family Placement Managers who completed some of the questionnaire ɯɯ ɯɯ have the information.

A third of the authorities were satisfied with the visiting pattern, almost six out of ten indicated mixed or 'half and half' levels of satisfaction, with the remaining two being definitely dissatisfied. In explanatory comments and in interviews some managers said: 'not as many as we would like'; 'some social workers are excellent but others seldom visit'; 'satisfied usually'; or ' increased access and understanding would be helpful'.

Explanations offered for differences found in placement workers' and social workers' performance

With very few exceptions, managers were not surprised to hear of the service gaps and of the higher appreciation expressed by carers towards family placement workers, compared to children's social workers. If there was a surprise, it was that more carers had not expressed higher levels of dissatisfaction with the social workers' activities. As one of them remarked:

Considering the pressures they are under this is not bad at all. I thought it would be another horror finding about social workers.

Some managers added that social workers themselves would not be surprised to hear of the carers' views. Most of the identified problems were explained as being largely due to shortage of resources and the many other demands made on the social worker's time. They referred to social workers as being: 'overwhelmed', 'overstretched', 'submerged' and sometimes 'stressed with the number of child protection cases and emergencies they have to attend to'.

It was not the first time during this stage of the study that child protection and emergency work undertaken by social workers were singled out by managers as being mainly responsible for most of the limitations of the fostering service. An often repeated comment was:

The social worker is often glad to have a safe place for the child.
Or
Once children are in placement, social workers have no time to pursue visits and plans and a drift can follow.

Four authorities, in their efforts to cope with the high number of child protection investigations and assessments, had set up specialist child protection teams. Yet three of the four managers from these authorities said that they saw no difference in the way children's social workers operated because the overall resources had remained unchanged or most of the resources had followed the child protection teams. It was further reported that, in a number of authorities, cases of children remained unallocated because of unfilled vacancies. Butler and Charles (1999) also found that direct work with children and young people was inhibited by organisational cutbacks.

Other explanations offered included: ambiguity over who works with the child and who provides support to the carers in relation to the child.

Role delineation of who did what, and especially who was "in charge", were said by a number of managers to be a grey or ambiguous area. When managers were asked to say which of the two types of worker carers should turn to in times of emergencies or crises connected with the child's behaviours and circumstances, the answers varied between placement and children's social workers. Some managers reported that carers frequently turned to family placement workers because they knew the latter better or that social workers were unavailable or that some did not know the children well enough:

It is the link worker who has a close affinity with the foster carers and learns more about the child; some social workers never get to know the child.

154

Uncertainty about who is meant to provide support to carers in relation to the child epitomises also the problem of who is meant to act as their first line manager and who is to provide supervision to them and what supervision should be about.

Mixed attitudes towards carers

While the majority of social workers were said to be appreciative and often 'grateful' to carers for taking the children in, very often at a moment's notice, apparently a small minority displayed mixed feelings or negative stereotypes about them. Social workers' attitudes reported by managers included 'always wanting things', 'always expecting visits', 'always asking for grants', 'always wanting more and more support', and 'they are now "professionals" and should be getting on with the job'.

One manager made the remark that 'carers feel they always have to ask for everything and social workers feel that carers are always wanting'.

How unrealistic were the carers in their expectations of support and visits? An examination of carer handbooks revealed strong encouragement to them by the agency to make full use of the services of the child's social worker and 'never to hesitate to get in touch'. If anything, it was the manuals and possibly preparation and training that raised the carers' expectations. As one handbook says:

Social workers are there to help and advise. Please use them. Do not hesitate to get in touch if you are worried about something, even if it may seem trivial.

The lack of specialist training in fostering

The lack of fostering expertise on the part of 'many' social workers was commented upon by both managers and carers. Even though most of the social workers worked in child care teams, it did not always follow that they were also all knowledgeable about matters relevant to fostering or had skills in direct work with children.

Social workers are monitoring their (children's) activities, rather than undertaking direct work with them.

With one exception, all authorities said that they had a requirement that all staff working in child care should have training on the subject.

However, only a third of authorities indicated that they had a requirement that social workers should also be familiar with fostering work. The higher turnover, we were told, of children's social workers compared to placement workers, only accentuated the problem. Similarly, in small authorities a worker might not have enough, or any cases, for some time to enable them to develop enough expertise in foster care.

As an example of the neglect of this aspect of child care, of the 37 post-qualifying and advanced courses approved by CCETSW across the UK in relation to children and families, 25 were in child protection and only two in family placement work. The remaining 10 were courses in general child welfare or child care work (see *The PQ Directory*, Central Council for Education and Training in Social Work, London, 1997).

Tensions between the two parts of the fostering service

Over a third of the managers completing the questionnaire agreed that there were some tensions between children's social workers and placement workers. It was also claimed that on occasions difficulties that arose between social workers and carers spilled over into the relationships between placement workers and social workers. Some of the tensions seemed to arise from the type of perceptions each had of the other and these are outlined in Table 11.6.

Table 11.6

Perceptions attributed to the placement service and to child care teams about each other

Placement service/link workers	Child care teams/children's social worker
• a protected and cushioned elite	• failing to provide the comprehensive assessment reports needed for matching
• out of touch with the demands made on area teams	• not responding to carers' requests for support in relation to the children and not valuing carers
• failing to provide the family placement resources when needed	• not being easily available for co-ordination meetings and consultation
• being over-protective of carers and failing to see their weaknesses	• lack of fostering knowledge and expertise

Co-ordination and management

Both carers and managers referred to a lack of concerted co-ordination and communication between placement staff and children's social workers. Collaboration was made more difficult by the physical separation in the majority of authorities of the two parts of the service, separate line management, and the amount of work coming in, which meant that social workers and link workers were frequently occupied with few opportunities for consultation and co-ordination. Sometimes, these two types of worker did not meet each other except at reviews, though they could communicate by other means.

The identification of some serious gaps in service provision connected with the role of the child's social worker could easily result in the authors looking for a convenient scapegoat. While placement workers have developed a close alliance with carers, this has not been the case with children's social workers. No doubt much more remains to be done in this direction, but it also has to be recognised that the role of the children's social worker in relation to the child and the carers is a more complex and conflictual one than that of the placement worker. It was rightly argued that priority for children's social workers are the needs, welfare, safety and rights of the child, rather than support to carers, though the two need not be mutually exclusive.

SUMMARY

- Placement workers and children's social workers carry most of the responsibility for delivering the fostering service.
- In a third of the authorities, the role of the child's social worker in relation to the child and the carers had not been defined in writing and in many others it was poorly defined leading to many ambiguities and uncertainties.
- Significant differences in carer satisfaction were found between the role and work of the placement worker and that of the child's social worker, in favour of the former.
- Carers who were unhappy about the availability of the social worker and or frequency of visits also: found the children more difficult than expected; found that their expectations of fostering were not met;

thought about giving up fostering; needed a break/respite; and said that the department could do more for its carers.

- While, on the whole, carers give the fostering service their approval, there are also a number of problematic areas requiring urgent attention. They include frequency of visits, availability, support and appreciation. These were found to be associated with finding the children more difficult than expected; expectations not having been met; thinking about giving up; and that the department could do more for its carers.

- Those fostering for a special scheme/drawing a fee were more likely to be satisfied than the rest.

- Foster carers rated placement workers attached to units higher than those based in area teams.

- On the whole, service managers confirmed the main service gaps identified by carers concerning infrequent visits, non-availability and poor support mainly by the child's social worker.

- Tensions were identified between child care area teams and the family placement part of the fostering service.

- With one exception, all authorities expected the child's social worker to have training in child care but only a third expected familiarity with fostering work.

12 Assessments, matching and agreements

A number of interrelated activities permeate the early stages of fostering placement: the assessment of the carers and that of the child and the matching of child to carer. How these tasks are performed by authorities is the subject of this chapter.

TOWARDS A FRAMEWORK FOR ASSESSMENT AND MATCHING

A key concept surrounding matching is that placement decisions should aim to fit the children's assessed developmental, religious, racial, ethnic, cultural and language needs and the assessed skills and family circumstances of foster carers. However, in spite of the centrality of matching in planning placement work for children, two recent reviews of the fostering research literature seem to have identified no studies of direct relevance to the subject (Sellick and Thoburn, 1996; Berridge, 1997). The two people exercising a pivotal role in the matching process are the placement worker who knows the carers and the social worker who knows the child.

i) Assessment of foster carers
All the authorities had in place assessment systems which aimed, among other things, to establish the specific strengths, skills and competencies of carers. Though the carers' general qualities are assessed at the point of selection, these have also to be considered again in relation to the specific needs and circumstances of the child to be placed. Consultation with carers about their placement preferences was the responsibility of placement staff, except in the few authorities where area team staff combined the role of both child's social worker and placement worker. Much more detailed consultation, we found, was likely to take place in relation to long term and so called "permanent" or "planned" placements, than with other types.

Carer preferences

Carers, we found, had specific preferences, especially in relation to the child's age (58 per cent) and then his/her sex (32 per cent). Others wanted the kind of child that would fit in with their family or work commitments or with what they perceived themselves to be good at. Some of the carers' specifications about sex preferences had mainly to do with fears about allegations of sexual abuse. Around a fifth wanted a child younger than their own because they did not want the foster child to dominate their own. We saw in an earlier chapter that there are certain risks when the placed child is older to an own by less than five years. Almost one in ten with a preference felt that a specific age group, especially older children, would fit in with their work patterns. Accommodation considerations were also important in influencing preferences. In interviews, a few carers also said that fostering teenagers meant having fewer "hassles" with parents because teenagers could arrange for contact away from the foster home.

Of carers who expressed an age preference, over a fifth wanted a child under the age of five with another fifth expressing a preference for 0–10-year-olds (a fifth of under five-year-olds in the sample were fostered by carers aged 51–60). A quarter were definitely interested in 5–10 year olds and the rest, approximately a third, were interested in adolescents and young people.

Table 12.1
Preferred age group

Age group	Preference	
	N	*%*
0–4	107	22
0–10	91	19
5–10	117	25
5–15	27	6
11+	131	28
Total	**473***	**100**

*Some carers gave no details of their preferences.

Teenagers and gay young people

Three-fifths of carers indicated that they would be prepared to foster a teenager but only a quarter of all carers said they would consider fostering a gay teenager. Those over the age of 40 were more likely to indicate willingness to foster teenagers, but less likely to foster a gay teenager. Again there were variations between authorities. Four out of five carers in one agency were prepared to consider fostering a teenager, against 29 per cent in another.

Over 90 per cent of carers said that their wishes were taken into account for the last placement they had. This seems to be a high percentage of fulfilled preferences when the shortage of placements is considered and the pressure carers come under to take almost any child. On the other hand, almost a fifth of placement-vacancies remained unused, partly because carer preferences could not be met.

ii) Assessment of the child's needs and circumstances

The assessment of looked after children was mainly the responsibility of area team social workers aided, where necessary, by input from outside professionals.

In-house assessment

The most likely person to carry out the child's assessment was the family's social worker. This worker usually, but not always, knew the child beforehand and also carried case responsibility. Others from the area team who happened to know the family or child might also be asked to contribute to this assessment. Usually an assessment report had to be specially prepared for the fostering purpose. Where an assessment report on the child had already been prepared for the panel/court, this would also accompany the request for a placement or sometimes be supplemented to take account of the fostering requirements.

The literature on assessment expects that information gathered by social workers during their interviews will use a suitable framework for analysing it. The study found that it was less likely for authorities to use a standard assessment framework for emergency fostering and more likely to use one for medium and long-term placements. Even with medium and long-term fostering referrals, one in every four authorities was not using an assessment framework at all. Reliance was apparently placed on each worker using his/her own framework and on the exchange of information by phone or after the placement was made. (At the time the study was carried out, the Looking After Children schedules had not yet been implemented in Scotland.)

External input

Outside contributions to assessment were likely to be sought from teachers, especially for children referred to a children's hearing system, followed by doctors and then educational psychologists. Psychiatrists were also used, but more rarely. External input was more likely to be sought for a report to the panel/court than for one going straight to the fostering placement team or residential care team. One major reason why psychiatric and psychological reports were less routinely asked for was the amount of time it took to obtain them.

Expectations of assessment reports

Irrespective of whether an authority used an assessment framework or not, placement workers, who were responsible for finding the placements and shared the matching responsibility with children's social workers and carers, expected detailed information on each child to enhance their understanding. As one of them put it:

> It is important to know about contact, schooling, behaviours, expectations of carers. It is not enough for social workers to say that their expectation is simply for carers to look after a child.

The views of other professionals, mainly from education and health, would be incorporated in the report, along with any available psychological or psychiatric reports. Finally, a recommendation was expected from the social worker about the kind of placement needed, for how long and expectations of it.

A number of grey areas, however, surrounded these expectations, depending on how a placement was classified e.g. emergency, temporary, planned or permanent. On the whole, less information was expected for temporary placements than for permanent. Furthermore, while in some authorities the term "temporary" was used to cover emergency and short-term placements only, in others it also covered medium-term ones. Similar ambiguities surrounded the terms "planned" and "unplanned" used in some other authorities. This meant that, for children going into "non-permanent" or "unplanned" placements, that is, the majority, a number of authorities were not requiring detailed assessment reports before the placement was made. As one service manager described it:

Matching is only attempted in permanent placements, otherwise it is a telephone call from the child's social worker based on sketchy information.

Satisfaction with reports

Around half the managers were satisfied with the quality of the reports they obtained from their respective child care teams. Some of the satisfied service managers said things like:

We manage to get a reasonable level of information but I often have to chase it up.

Service managers who were dissatisfied made many references to the absence of detail that they felt was essential for matching purposes:

Even where the child and the family have been known quite well we get very poor information. We have a lot of conflict over this with the child care team.

The Census (Chapter 7) identified that over half of placements were made as emergencies, which meant that no meaningful matching could take place beforehand. As an example, one authority which organised around 40 "emergency" placements over the census period could provide no information on the particular needs of a single child. A couple of service managers were determined to return unsatisfactory reports, but this was neither universal nor always easy. Such an insistence, it was said, would only add to the already identified difficulties and tensions between area teams and the fostering placement service. One manager summed it up as follows:

The child is in a safe place with a foster mum and it's a relief. The impetus then to gather information or to work on the plan's fine details gets lost a bit, at least for several weeks, until there is a review point.

Based on the overall evidence obtained, it does appear that the assessment of many children was rather unsystematic and so was the collection of background information for matching purposes. These findings help also to explain why so many carers complained about not getting adequate information on the child's background.

iii) Location of placements

On the whole, authorities were anxious to avoid placing children too far from their neighbourhood to help maintain the links with their families and friends. This presented special problems in rural areas where the placements were not always where they were wanted and partly accounted for almost a fifth of placements not being used. Similar considerations also applied to some city authorities that relied heavily on placements outside their boundaries.

iv) Consulting children and parents

Almost nine out of ten authorities said that they consulted the child or young person about the placement. Almost without exception, this responsibility fell exclusively on the children's social workers. Preferences and wishes would mostly be ascertained through talking and discussions, but on occasions more imaginative ways were used, such as drawings. It was not perhaps surprising also to be told that consulting, especially younger children, was an unsystematic and infrequent process. Some typical comments included: 'Children's views not asked' or 'Children's views are not sought enough'.

Again, consultation with children was said to be mostly confined to what were described as 'permanent', 'long-term' or 'planned' placements.

The children's social workers were also expected to consult with parents before requesting a placement, but the study was unable to obtain specific information on how satisfactorily this was done. The drawing up of agreements was meant to give parents the opportunity for a more active participation but the general view conveyed was that, until now, this form of consultation varied.

v) Ethnicity, race, culture, language, religion and class

Most authorities subscribed to the idea of ethnic and racial matching, and to specific language and religious matching. Though barely two per cent of black/minority ethnic children in Scotland at any one time require ethnic and/or racial matching, nevertheless, as we have found, these aims were rarely realisable because recruitment of carers to reflect the children's ethnic needs was lagging very much behind. As we have seen in Chapter 7 on Supply and Demand, almost half the authorities in Scotland and three-fifths in England said they experienced 'serious' problems in finding placements that reflected black/minority ethnic children's backgrounds.

The study did not obtain information on whether matching by class was being pursued or not. However, with well over a quarter of female foster carers in the study being classified in the two top social classes and another quarter as non-manual, matching in terms of class would have been often impossible. We do not know the exact impact on foster children of being cared for in families which perceive themselves as well functioning and in many ways different and as providing a superior environment to that of the children's families (see also Butler and Charles, 1999). A summary of recent English adoption research noted that social class was not important as a variable contributing to breakdowns in arrangements (Parker, 1999) but, of course, unlike those fostered, adopted children are not meant to return to their birth families.

vi) A pool of carers

One assumption usually made is that staff will be able to match children's needs with carers from an available pool who have different skills and competencies. The House of Commons Health Committee Report (1998) also stressed the necessity for each local authority to have a surplus capacity of placements at all times in order for real choice to be exercised, though this capacity did not currently exist (p 35).

At the time of the study, 17 per cent of placements were unused, suggesting the existence of a sizeable pool of carers offering matching choices to staff. However, this figure was rather deceptive. Most of these vacancies remained unfilled due to carers' preference for specific children or because they lived in areas where they were least needed.

The study asked a number of questions about the availability of placements for different types of fostering and the replies are set out below (see also discussion on supply and demand in Chapter 7).

Emergency and short-term placements

As seen from Table 12.2, there are many similarities between Scotland and England when it comes to choice of placements for emergency and short-term placements, albeit the situation for Scotland is somewhat worse.

Ability to choose a placement from two or three was unusual, especially for children over 10. In fact, no authority in Scotland and only three per cent in England said they were able to 'almost always' offer such choice to those over 10 and around six out of ten said 'rarely'. The situation was somewhat better with under ten-year-olds for whom seven to eight authorities in both countries said they were able to offer choice either 'always' or 'sometimes'.

Table 12.2

In emergency and unplanned short-term admissions to foster care are social workers usually able to offer a choice of placement?

	Children under 10		Children over 10	
	Scotland %	England* %	Scotland %	England* %
Almost always	19	19	–	3
Sometimes	50	65	32	38
Rarely	31	16	68	59
Total	**100**	**100**	**100**	**100**

Waterhouse (1997).

Chapter 7 on Supply and Demand also identified the main groups in both Scotland and England who were least likely to be placed because of placement shortages. It included: older children, sibling groups, minority ethnic children, those with difficult behaviour, those requiring long-term placements and children with disabilities.

In many managers' views, matching was unrealisable because of lack of placement choices and the lack of resources for more detailed work to be undertaken including the assessment of children. The most that could be expected was a "safe" place for the child. Typical comments included: 'lack of choice, lack of carers', 'shortage of carers', 'lack of time to assess the children's needs', 'shortage of carers especially for sibling groups and teenagers', 'problem of supply and demand particularly for 10+', 'lack of resources', 'too many emergencies', 'no families for children with disabilities', and 'placements not in the right place and at the right time'.

These above views were confirmed in our earlier study in relation to placements for teenagers (Triseliotis *et al*, 1995a). Other studies have concluded that children are often placed where there is a vacancy rather than in an assessed placement suitable to meet their needs (Berridge and Cleaver, 1987; Strathclyde, 1988). More encouraging are our census findings, outlined in Chapter 7, which show that, of children placed, six out of every seven, in fact, went to first choice placements.

A further factor that contributed to placement shortages was apparently the 'unnecessary' extension of some placements because social workers did not have enough time to work directly with the children and their families, to speed up reunification or rehabilitation. In some new smaller authorities, there was less choice in matching some children's very special needs because of the small pool of carers, and inter-agency placements were proving difficult to negotiate. Furthermore, budget constraints made it equally difficult to access the non-statutory sector.

vii) The "fit" between child and carers

Wolkind and Rushton (1994) point out that placement outcome is highly related to the interaction and relationship that develops between the child and the carers. Yet, as some placement managers remarked, this is a "luxury" not afforded to them because placements are mostly made without the benefit of such observations. Trial periods for observation before finalising a placement were said to be rare. Reliance was placed instead on a review following the placement made and, if found wanting, the placement would be terminated. Terminating a placement, irrespective of how quickly this was done, was said to be very infrequent because of the complexities it would raise. As a result, placement staff relied heavily on the pattern of interactions established between carers and previous children they fostered and on the social worker's observation of the child in previous settings. (The census survey established that a fifth of the children were re-referrals.)

Who does the matching?

Theoretically, matching is meant to be a collective responsibility between the child's social worker, the placement worker and the carer, sometimes with the involvement of their respective line managers. In practice, and because of pressures of work and the high number of referrals, matching mainly became the responsibility of the placement worker and the child's social worker. More joint and planned decisions were likely to be taken in relation to long-term or so called "permanent" placements. Around a third of the Scottish authorities, and almost all English ones, expected their panels to take an active part in the matching of children to carers or at least to agree to the placement.

SUMMARY

- A framework for matching consisted of the following elements, though its systematic application varied: assessment and preferences of carers; assessment and needs of children; location of placements; consultation with parents and children; issues of ethnicity, race, culture, language, religion and class; and a pool of carers from which choices could be made. The "fit" between carers and child based on observed interactions was said to be unrealisable.
- On the whole, authorities had not developed yet clear standard expectations about assessment and matching, the process to be followed, and how decisions should be made and when. It was an area requiring urgent clarification. A clear matching framework was also lacking.
- Imprecise definitions obscured the numbers of children left without either proper assessment or matching.
- Teachers and doctors were the most likely professionals from outside social work to contribute fairly routinely to the assessment of children.

- Only half of managers surveyed were satisfied with the quality of assessment reports. Communications between area teams and placement staff on issues of assessment and matching were said to require improvement.
- No agency said that the matching of children to carers was fully realisable. Placements were mostly supply rather than needs-led. Matching was adversely affected by the shortage of carers for most types of need.
- On the whole "permanent" placements received greater attention than others.
- Eliciting the views and preferences of children, parents and carers for specific placements was unsystematic.

13 **The meaning of support**

The notion of support to foster carers and the child in foster care is a major feature of the fostering literature. We saw in earlier chapters how often carers were critical of authorities for failing to provide adequate support to the child and themselves. Most studies in foster care end with a recommendation for more support to be made available to foster carers and/or foster children. Sellick and Thoburn (1996) highlight three reasons why support to foster carers by authorities is crucial: firstly, it maximises their retention; secondly, it minimises agency costs; and thirdly, it prevents the breakdown of placements.

Two SSI Inspections of local authority fostering services in England found that 50 per cent of foster carers surveyed said they did not always feel they were well supported (House of Commons Health Committee Report, 1998, p 30). Another publication on the inspection of local authority services reported that foster carers were generally content with the support of their link workers but had low expectations of the support they might receive from children's social workers who were seen as 'unresponsive, inaccessible and administratively inept' (Department of Health, 1995). Witnesses told the House of Commons Health Committee (1998, p.31) that carers are tempted to "defect" from local authorities to independent fostering agencies not just because they offer higher fees but because they offer, or are believed to offer, a higher quality of support for carers. The report went on to urge local authorities to invest more resources in the training of foster carers, to ensure that link and support workers liaise with carers, and in practicalities like help with transport and insurance and to also investigate the possibility of setting up a pension scheme for foster carers (p 35).

There are only two British studies known to us which examined foster care outcomes in relation to support. Aldgate and Hawley (1986) concluded that fostering households who had experienced breakdowns were left to struggle on until they eventually reached a point of sheer desperation. More important, the Strathclyde fostering outcomes study

(1988 and 1991) disclosed a higher rate of 'premature endings of placements' where the social worker did not keep in regular contact. Though the nature of post-placement support in adoption is not exactly comparable with foster care because of the different expectations, nevertheless, a recent study was unable to establish a relationship between the level of social work support and the outcome of placements after a year (Quinton *et al*, 1997). The authors warn that it should not be concluded that support made no difference because many parents were appreciative of the help they had received. Another adoption study reported that adopters who had experienced disruptions felt that had they had more support the placement might have survived (Lowe *et al*, 1999).

In Chapter 11 it was reported how levels of support and some of its constituent bodies, such as frequency of visits and availability, were found by this study to be significantly linked to whether:

- the children were found to be more difficult than expected;
- expectations of fostering were met;
- carers contemplated stopping fostering; and
- carers needed respite.

Support is meant to be provided by the placement worker, the child's social worker, and the agency as a whole. In spite of its extensive use, detailed discussion of the meaning and components of support has been limited (see Triseliotis *et al*, 1995a). This chapter draws together the key dimensions in service delivery identified by carers and whose consistent application constitutes support to the child and themselves.

SUPPORT AND ITS CONSTITUENT COMPONENTS

Carers came into fostering with a number of expectations from the service and many of these were reinforced during preparation and training. In some ways these expectations became the yardstick by which to judge the performance of the fostering services. They had mainly to do with a range of activities carried out by the agency and its staff which carers collectively associated with support. As described by many carers, this involves a range of practices, attitudes and resources that have to go hand in hand.

The word "support" has permeated much of this research so far as it featured as an answer to most of the themes connected with the operation of the fostering service. It also held centre stage in the personal interviews held with carers. Carers are often expected to care for difficult children requiring the deployment of special knowledge and skills. Chapters 8 and 14 have highlighted how the children's problems and the lack of support were the two major reasons for carers actually giving up fostering and for many others thinking about doing so.

What is meant by support can be ambiguous, contentious and can vary from one group to another. Many carers were anxious to stress that support was not one-dimensional or simply having someone to talk things over with. It went well beyond this and covered a range of other crucial components, some referring to themselves and others to direct work with the children, which are outlined later. The following is a typical comment by one carer:

Support is about availability, listening, understanding, and where necessary doing something about it such as suggesting alternative ways of doing things; providing honest information about the children and their families, not only rosy pictures. Training and going to conferences are also part of support and to have other expert help when needed.

Others put the emphasis on direct work and support to the foster children and the implications for them when this was not forthcoming. An earlier chapter on delivery highlighted many uncertainties within authorities of who was to provide support to the carers in relation to the child.

The constituent components of support

Almost three-fifths of all carers agreed or agreed strongly that the agency could do more in a number of areas of support. Leaving aside the issue of pay and conditions of service, which are discussed in Chapter 15, the rest of the package desired by carers comprised:

- more frequent social work visits mainly for direct input with the child;
- greater social work availability and reliability, including 24 hour cover;
- being listened to, valued and appreciated especially by the agency;

- working as a team/partnership, including full information on the children and their families;
- continued training, including more training and support over contact;
- parental visits and behaviours;
- more support for the whole family when children leave;
- support through false allegations; and
- more respite.

(Most of the above topics are discussed in other chapters and only selected reference will be made to them here.)

More frequent visits, especially by social workers

As expected, there were many positive experiences and much praise for the many children's social workers who provided support on a routine basis and who were there to be contacted if and when needed. These were expressed in comments such as: 'excellent relationships, the same for nine years'; or 'missed him when he left'; or 'we would give up if we ever lost the support of our social worker'. Other typical comments included:

Our social worker makes us feel we are doing really well for our foster child.

I am treated with respect for a job done well.

We saw in an earlier chapter, though, that frequency of visits by social workers was the least favourably rated dimension with only 21 per cent of carers describing it as 'very satisfactory'. Carers wanted themselves and the child to have regular contact with the child's social worker, in particular, quick access in times of emergencies and crisis. Routine contact was viewed as necessary on two counts: first, in the interests of the child who needed to develop a relationship of trust with a social worker. Many carers closely associated infrequent visits with the absence of 'direct input' with the child, which they felt was 'unfair to the child' and also to themselves because they had to make up for this deficiency. Examples were also given of some children barely knowing their social worker and, more rarely, of not having one at all. Typical comments included:

A lot of children do not get the emotional backing they need.

Secondly, carers also wanted regular contact with the same social worker, so that they could develop a working relationship, share in the planning, make contact arrangements for parents and, where necessary, engage in problem-solving. Preferably, this person had to be someone they knew and who knew the child:

Somebody you know truly understands. You cannot talk to friends about such things.

We have been told that, where there was a placement worker involved, some social workers saw it as their role to concentrate more on the needs of the parents than the foster carers. This further confirmed the view, in some carers' minds, that children's social workers were more interested in the natural parents than in the child or the carers.

A number of carers claimed that they had either no contact with their social worker unless they 'initiated it', or they met only at reviews. Many others resented the view that they were now seen as 'professionals' or that they were 'paid' for their work and 'should get on with it'. Some added that social workers were professionals and were paid but they still expected support from their seniors.

Availability

Alongside frequency of visits, availability of social workers also emerged as a major component of support. It was a theme around which many frustrations, and sometimes anger, were voiced. By availability carers meant both the social worker's availability and reliability and the authority's stand-by and emergency arrangements. As some carers put it, availability meant being able, when worried, to get in touch with a member of staff, preferably the child's social worker, to discuss the situation. The following are two of many similar comments:

Support is about phoning when you are worried about something and there is someone to talk it over. To let off steam. For someone to listen.

If you telephone, it means you are desperate otherwise you wouldn't do it.

Though many carers expressed high levels of satisfaction with the availability of their social workers, the frustrations and, often, anger of the rest have to be seen in the light of their own perception of their 24 hour commitment to the children. Anything less was considered to be unacceptable. A significant percentage of them said that they had great difficulty in establishing contact, mainly with the child's social worker. Worse was not having messages or calls returned. Comments included 'never available'; 'at a meeting'; 'not in'; 'messages not returned'; 'lack of communication'; 'most of them work on the 9 to 5 o'clock principle, but expect carers to be always available'; 'messages are not always passed on or not always returned'; or 'they have got a saying "I will get back to you on that, and they never do'.

Carers remarked on the lack of reliability of some children's social workers: 'not keeping appointments'; 'not arriving on time and not apologising for being late'; 'not ringing up to say he/she would be late arriving'; or 'not acting on promises'.

It was also a sign of reliability and valuing to return calls and messages and take action when promised. Reliability referred to behaviour both towards carers and children, with some carers giving examples of either themselves and/or the children being badly let down:

Letting the children down at the last moment is not acceptable.

Another image of social workers carried by a great number of carers is of people who are always unavailable when needed, either attending meetings or courses. A lack of response made some carers feel 'abandoned', 'isolated' and 'alone', interpreting unavailability as also a lack of concern for the children. It was claimed that some workers would go on holiday without naming a substitute contact. In interviews some carers drew contrasts between the agency's fostering manual urging them to get in touch with the social worker, whenever needed, with the difficulty of accessing him/her.

Feelings of isolation when problems arose could be alleviated, in the view of some, by having a helpline. Others added:

We need more support, more visits, phone calls, availability.

The worst periods, apparently, were weekends and holidays. If there was a crisis during such periods, some carers had to wait until the holiday or weekend was over before someone called back. Another aspect about availability concerned the expertise of those staffing the standby service. It was argued that they should be knowledgeable and experienced in fostering to understand and be able to offer suggestions.

Stand-by is manned by people who do not know the children and who have no understanding of the fostering issues. So not of much use.

Sellick (1992) found from his study that a key reason for why some carers moved to the independent sector was the 24 hour cover offered.

Carers acknowledged that support, especially during periods of crisis, could also come from other carers and family members, which was valued because of a shared understanding, but there were times when this was not enough. Some carers had established their own informal systems and the one voluntary agency featuring in the sample had developed a more formalised arrangement in some cases, which was very valued and highly praised. However, what mattered most in times of crisis was being able to talk to someone who carried authority and responsibility:

. . . to share the responsibility with the person responsible for the child and the plan.

Greater availability and more frequent visits were often accompanied by a call for social workers to develop much more expertise in direct work with children, especially in the management of unacceptable behaviours. They expected them to have more expertise to help children directly and equally to help carers to understand children's behaviours better and how to manage them. While learning more about children, carers also wanted social workers to use more 'common sense' by which they usually meant not being too soft or 'taken for a ride' by children: 'avoid being manipulated by children'; 'not always to side with the children'; 'see the carer's point of view'; 'not spoil them with too many treats'; recognise the need 'for firm boundaries'; or 'avoid taking children's rights to extremes'.

Part-time staff

Though carers showed understanding of why some staff have to work part-time, they were not certain that fostering was the right place for them to be because of their unavailability during periods of crisis. Staff standing in for them were not always considered knowledgeable enough about the circumstances of the individual case to be of much help. Some tended to contrast, unfavourably, part-time work with their own 'round the clock' commitment:

As she is part-time, she is not always there when you need her.

This poses a challenge to management to arrange the work of part-time staff in a way that does not compromise continuity of service.

Being listened to, understood, appreciated, valued and involved

Besides concrete aspects of support such as pay, frequency of visits and availability, much emphasis was also placed on the intangible aspects of support. This came in the form of a 'relationship', being 'listened to', 'understood' and 'taken seriously', especially when there were difficulties in the placement. We have seen earlier that social workers, link workers, but not the agency, were given good ratings on listening and appreciation, but when asked what more the department could do, or what they would like to teach social workers, listening to carers and more valuing and appreciation were very high on their agendas:

No appreciation; no listening; no understanding.

An SSI report also found that two-thirds of carers surveyed in some authorities in England felt that social workers did not listen to their views (quoted by the House of Commons Health Committee Report, 1998). It was felt by many carers in the present study that some workers and managers were failing to appreciate the stresses, the 'emotional draining' and physical 'exhaustion' involved in fostering. As a result, a minority of the children's social workers, and sometimes the agency, drew much criticism and adverse comments from these carers. A sample of more negative comments included: 'over-bearing attitude'; 'patronising'; 'looking down on you'; or 'not taking our word'.

Inevitably, a number of carers experienced what they described as 'good' and 'bad' workers, the latter being in a minority. Some of the criticisms came also from generally satisfied carers, who nevertheless felt that they were not being listened to, or not being understood and that their experience and observations about the child were not valued by the social worker or management. A few carers said that they had to make a real fuss before getting support or getting clothes for the children or the child referred for specialist help:

You have to make a fuss to get support. It shouldn't be like that.

There were times when listening, though experienced as supportive, was by itself not enough. Some carers would have liked more action, such as being given a break, the child being referred for more specialist help or to a group, or for some kind of activity to be arranged for the child. Social workers and link workers have to understand each carer and each situation individually and judge when it is appropriate simply to listen, which can be supportive, and when more action is needed. As an example, the comment 'you are doing well' may be experienced as supportive and valuing by one carer, but as patronising by another, depending on the context within which it takes place.

A number of carers were anxious to shift criticism from their social workers to management. They felt that social workers were on the whole good at listening and understanding, but that it was the policies which were at fault. This might have to do with the way planning and decisions were arrived at, or the amount of resources made available and the way this influenced the overall time social workers had for visits and support. Almost half the carers, more in some authorities than others, felt that management was distant and that the carers' expectations of support and related issues were not getting through. Differences over single payments and delays over pay contributed to further bad feeling.

The absence of closer contacts between senior management and carers, or their representatives, increased the feelings of distance and of 'a bureaucracy at work'. Such feelings were accentuated in some authorities where it was felt that too many people were involved without it being clear who carried overall responsibility. This feeling made some carers once again raise the question of commitment but now in relation to the agency:

The administrative bureaucracy sees children as pieces of paper, not as children who need love and care.

Overall, authorities and staff have a real task on their hands over how to make carers feel better understood, valued and appreciated so as to improve their level of rapport with the whole agency and not solely with individual staff members. Such an expectation should not be seen as unusual. Improved and continuing training could also promote self-approval and assist carers to have more confidence in their own abilities, possibly helping to raise, at the same time, their level of tolerance of unusual behaviours displayed by the children.

Working as a team or in partnership

The word "partnership" has featured a lot in the social work literature of the last ten years or so and in guidance to recent child care legislation. Social workers and the social work services are urged to work "in partnership" with the users of the service and especially the parents of children who need looking after. Appropriately, the word "partnership" has also entered the fostering literature urging social workers and carers to work together "in partnership" or pursue team-work and to aim for colleague-type relationships. In the case of service users, it may be unrealistic to talk of a 'relationship of equality' because of the power differentials, but this should be less so in the case of foster carers who are colleagues.

Partnership, like support, is based on a range of behaviours on the part of staff of the fostering services and the department, rather than on single actions. In the carers' eyes it covers such items as:

* joint planning and decision making;
* assessing and matching children to carers;
* sharing/exchanging information on all aspects;
* participation in the recruitment, selection, preparation and continued training of new carers; and
* being represented on management and policy making committees.

Many carers observed that team-work or partnership may have been talked about more than practised. The emerging view was that as an idea it was not properly built into the workings or structures of the agency. As a result it relied largely on the commitment of the individual social worker and placement worker. Some carers would say:

We should have more say in what happens to the children.

Or

Treat us as part of the team all the time.

Many carers made indirect reference to team-work by using words and phrases which either suggested that they were being treated as "partners" or the opposite. Some examples included: 'be treated as equal'; 'work together'; ' to be consulted about plans'; 'seen as second class'; 'looked down upon'; 'them and us'; 'be seen as a colleague'; 'to be treated with respect'; 'they think they know it all'; 'not being listened to' or 'we are being used'.

A number of carers talked very positively and warmly about their experiences of team work with the fostering service. They spoke of their views being 'sought and respected', of 'being valued', of 'being listened to at reviews', of feeling 'equal' or of being treated 'as a full member of the team':

Everybody treated us as partners and were prepared to listen and we felt valued.

A recent study of foster carers in Fife also found that the most common plea was for more frequent visits from the children's social workers and an increased involvement in case planning (Ramsay, 1996).

Reviews

Reviews and what happened at them were seen as a further test of how much carers felt that their participation and contribution were valued and how they felt respected as equal members of the team. Reviews were also the place where carers mostly came in touch with more senior management. Irrespective of where reviews were held, these were experienced on the whole as 'helpful' and 'useful' by the majority and less so by others. Those satisfied with the way reviews were conducted would say: 'Very useful'; 'we learnt a lot from them and we were listened to'; 'problems were aired'; 'we got other people's views, including parents'; 'our views were listened to and valued'.

A minority of carers felt less positive about reviews and their participation:

> *Carers' views at reviews were at the end of the line. However, there were valuable contributions from teachers and health visitors who knew the children.*

It suited a number of carers to have the reviews at their home, especially those with very young children, when transport and child-minding arrangements would have presented problems. Other carers, however, felt differently. There was a widely held view that using the carers' homes for reviews signified further intrusion into their space and a loss of control. There was some resentment too that their home was being used like an office or a residential establishment.

> *You are left with no privacy. People going and coming like an office.*

Better communication and more information

The lack of background information on the children appeared repeatedly in the carers' comments and how this handicapped them in their caring and handling of the children. Failure to pass on background information was another example which conveyed to carers that they were not considered as full members of the team. Yet the Orkney Inquiry (1992) recommended that carers should be given written information on the children's background. This has now been incorporated into the Fostering of Children (Scotland) Regulations 1996. The main effect of "withholding" information, it was argued, was that carers were unable to understand or explain some children's behaviours, contribute at reviews, or be able to answer questions when taking a child to the doctor. Carers made comments about: 'being kept in the dark about the child's problems'; 'not being told about plans for the children'; 'not being wholly true about the child's background'; 'withholding the episodes of sexual abuse' or social workers needing to be 'more open and honest with the relevant facts'.

181

Other studies have also suggested that carers were inadequately informed (Vernon and Fruin, 1986); infrequently involved in discussions or planning and excluded from decision-making and not treated as partners (Waterhouse, 1992); and omitted from case conferences and reviews (Sinclair, 1984). When it comes to the sharing of background information on the children, Barth and Berry (1988) concluded from their adoption study that, when not informed in advance, families had particular difficulty adjusting to children who had been sexually abused or who had serious behaviour problems. Carers in the present study called for more 'honesty', 'greater openness', 'more sharing' or 'honesty and truthfulness':

The child's history – never hide anything from carers.

Few authorities said they allowed carers part or full access to children's case files, though copies of background reports were usually made available to them. Many managers were uncertain about how much information social workers and placement workers should disclose to carers and how to give information without breaking confidentiality. In their view, the needs of the carers to know conflicted, sometimes, with the right of the child, the child's family or of third parties to confidentiality. The policy in these authorities was to pass on information that directly related to the child, the care plans, medical reports, copies of assessment reports and review records. A few authorities were prepared to be more flexible on the matter, saying it depended 'on the circumstances' or 'the nature of the placement'. Several authorities, though, stressed that 'carers had no right of access' and only relevant reports could be made available.

Some carers suggested that, because of the quick turnover of social workers in some areas, some workers did not know the child enough to be able to share information or help in problem-solving. Not surprisingly, continuity of workers was highly valued. On the whole we had infinitely more good examples of co-operation and working together with staff known to carers for some time, than exasperation about someone being there for too long and blocking new developments.

Parental visits and behaviours

We saw in Chapter 10 that many foster carers experienced difficulties in handling parental contact. More guidance and support are needed to enable them to manage this aspect of their role. Carers are rightly asked to work in partnership with the children's parents, but it must be difficult for them to do this if they do not have a positive model with the authority of what partnership is about. What is perceived as supportive by carers with regard to contact are:

(a) clearer agreements about purpose and frequency of contact; where and when parents and children meet, who takes the child to meet their parents and whether the presence of a social worker will be necessary or not.

(b) The deployment of mediation type skills to help reconcile the two parties when disputes arise between carers and parents.

Many of the above arrangements should ideally feature in the placement agreement between the agency and the carers.

When foster children leave

The wider issues involved when children leave were discussed in Chapter 9. Suffice it to say here that what carers perceived as supportive in this case was for:

- better preparation on how to let children go;
- clearer expectations of each placement and better planning of the length of time each placement is expected to last;
- greater acknowledgement of the sense of loss experienced by carers and their families;
- well planned post-ending support; and
- the provision of feedback and, where appropriate, the maintenance of links.

Respite

There is a practical side to the idea of support. Opportunities for breaks or respite are one way of demonstrating this. Carers are often asked to take in children and to offer their parents some respite. Not surprisingly, it is something that they also expect for themselves. Yet only two authorities appeared to have a clear policy on the matter, even though the policy was not always followed through.

We have seen in different parts of the study how carers highlighted the amount of stress, burn-out and tiredness associated with fostering and hence the need for breaks 'to recharge batteries'. For example, 23 per cent gave stress/tiredness as the worst aspect of fostering, almost one in ten either actually gave up because of stress or were often or sometimes thinking about doing so. Around a third gave stress as the main reason for having a break.

SUMMARY

- The way carers understand support to themselves and the foster children matches with the kind of expectations they have before starting to foster. These are usually reinforced during preparation and by manuals, but not always matched up in practice.
- Some of the components of the support package, such as frequency of visits, availability, standby support over 24 hours, respite, clarity about entitlements and efficiency with payments are concrete and rely on the availability of resources. Others, such as listening, valuing, appreciation, answering messages and recognition of feelings of loss, are more intangible and rely on the attitudes and manners of staff.
- Support is perceived by carers as a package that has to be applied uniformly and consistently. Even levels of pay and the agency's efficiency in making arrangements for the carers' pay were viewed by some in the context of support. Applying only some parts of the package would not be addressing the problem in its entirety.

14 Foster carers who ceased to foster

The focus of this chapter is on foster carers who think of giving up fostering and of those who actually do give up voluntarily. In the process, comparisons are made between those carers who gave up and those who continued to foster. (At the suggestion of the agencies we left out those carers they had de-registered.)

BACKGROUND

Despite the long history of formal fostering in Britain, no systematic study had been carried out over the years to ascertain the rate of annual losses incurred when carers leave the service and to establish the reasons for this. The only published research known to us on the matter is what came to be known as the 'Portsmouth study' carried out more than 20 years ago (Jones, 1975) and Gregg's (1993) study also based on samples drawn from a single agency in England. Cliffe and Berridge (1991) reported high numbers of carers ceasing to foster but exact figures were missing. In addition, Pasztor and Wynne (1995) provide a summary of American studies on the subject. The dearth of studies in this area is illustrated by the fact that recent reviews of foster care research make only sparse reference to carer losses (Sellick and Thoburn, 1996; Berridge, 1997).

Knowing the former carers' views of why they ceased to foster, although only one of a number of aspects that have to be taken into account, nevertheless provides valuable feedback for authorities in developing their fostering services.

This study

The methods for identifying the sample and collecting information for this part of the study were discussed in the introductory chapter. Identifying exact figures of who ceased to foster and why was far from straightforward. Not all of the sampled authorities had accurate lists of those who ceased, or if they had, the lists did not always give the reasons why these had stopped fostering. Furthermore, modern systems of information technology had hardly been used to keep up-to-date information on issues of supply and demand, foster carer availability, preferences, and so on. The implications for policy making, planning and monitoring arising from the absence of such basic information are obvious.

After a rather complex and laborious process, including tapping the memories of staff, we were able to piece together what we think is a reliable picture of those who ceased to foster in 1994 and 1995 and why. We are confident that, in relation to two-thirds of the authorities featuring in the study, we were able to obtain fully accurate information. With the remaining one-third, we may be over or underestimating losses by about one per cent. Altogether information was obtained about the personal characteristics of the carers and their attitudes towards the fostering services. We were also able to examine differences and similarities with the sample of the active carers.

THINKING OF GIVING UP?

Before analysing and describing the characteristics and experiences of carers who gave up fostering, it is helpful to consider the views of current carers who had not given up fostering and then whether they themselves had thought, or were thinking, of doing so.

Above all, carers thought that the absence of social work support, the attitudes of some social workers, and increasing social work demands were the main reasons why other carers gave up. These were followed by burn-out and tiredness arising from hard work, the children's behaviours and problems, financial considerations, and the wish for more time for their own family and more privacy.

Around half the carers indicated that they themselves had either never or only infrequently thought of giving up fostering. At the other end, one in ten thought of this often and the rest (38 per cent) sometimes. In all, almost half of current carers think either 'often' or 'sometimes' of giving up fostering. Those who sometimes thought of giving up ranged from 73 per cent in one authority to 27 per cent in another. Single carers, female carers aged over 50, and carers with less than five years fostering experience were less likely to think of giving up fostering.

Carers who often or sometimes thought of giving up were asked to describe the circumstances that led them to feel like this. Though there was a diversity of responses to this question, some stood out from the rest and are outlined in Table 14.1.

Table 14.1
Why around half the carers 'often' or 'sometimes' felt like giving up

Reason	N *	%
Children's problems/mismatch	192	51
Lack of social work support	106	28
Social workers' attitudes/ideas	87	23
Burnt-out	62	16
Effect on own family	61	16
Attitudes of social work department	45	12
Allegations	42	11
Feeling inadequate	36	10
Financial	32	8
Parental interference	30	8
Other	21	5
Total	**714**	

*Some carers gave more than one reason.

The explanations offered by the 50 per cent or so of carers of why they 'often' or 'sometimes' thought of giving up fostering provide important clues about recruitment and retention. The following quotations illustrate the main reasons involved:

- *the children's behaviours*
  The children being far more difficult than expected making you feel inadequate.

- *absence of social work and departmental support*
  When you need help from social workers and you cannot get them. Poor back-up at nights and week-ends.

- *social work and management attitudes*
  Too many critical social workers and not enough sensitivity.

Frustration at not being listened to and undervalued.

- **effect on own family**
  My children becoming involved in the behaviours of the foster children.

- **stress and burn out**
  When you feel you have given everything you can emotionally and physically and they reject you leaving you drained.

Why did these carers not give up?

The predominant reason given by current carers for not giving up was either their 'fondness' and 'liking' for the current child (37 per cent) or the awareness of the pressing need for foster carers (33 per cent). Well behind were: remembering the positives, a sense of duty/obligation, sleeping over it and making a new start, and talking about it, mainly with their link worker, or other carers. A small number (seven per cent) said that they liked the job and the financial rewards that went with it. With this in mind, a few carers mentioned their mortgage. Predominantly it was attachment to the child and/or concern for the child which outweighed impulses to give up. Typical comments included 'fondness for current child'; 'the thought of the child going into a home'; 'we couldn't send our placements away'; or 'knowing how much I get out of it'.

FOSTER CARERS WHO GAVE UP

The point was made in Chapter 7 on supply and demand that the actual loss of carers in Scotland was less than expected at around seven per cent in the year April 1996 to March 1997. Only slightly higher proportions were found in England.

Background characteristics

The study contrasted a number of personal and background character-istics shared by former and continuing carers such as marital status, number of own children, religion, housing, ethnicity, health, educational qualifications, employment and social class. No significant differences were found between those who ceased to foster and active carers, except

that those who stopped were more likely to:
- have poorer health at the time of giving up (female carers);
- have somewhat larger families and more own dependent children;
- be active worshippers (female);
- hold non-manual occupations (female);
- have larger houses.

Unlike Jones (1975), this study found no significant differences between age at recruitment and ceasing to foster. Inevitably, studies such as Jones' based on single authorities simply show what is happening in that agency and findings cannot be generalised.

Motivation to foster

When it came to their stated motivation to foster, no discernible differences could be identified between former and continuing carers; the same concerns and interests had attracted both. Even certain differences found between female and male carers that were identified in the active group persisted within the group which ceased to foster.

Overall, and except for those who enter fostering with a view to adoption or because it suits their family's circumstances at a particular point and time, looking at the carers' motives as a key reason for ceasing to foster does not appear to be a productive line of enquiry. It is possible that better methods of preparation and selection, in the last decade or so, have led to greater uniformity in the type of person who comes into fostering now.

The foster children

The study also contrasted the number and type of children fostered at any one time by current and former carers, the ages of the children, sibling groups, children with mental or physical disabilities fostered, type of fostering undertaken (including community care schemes for adolescents), difficulties presented by the children, breaks and holidays taken. No significant differences were again found except that former carers were more likely to:
- have been fostering under five-year-olds;
- have had fewer breaks;

- say that they were not undertaking the kind of fostering they preferred; and
- have had more difficulties with parents over contact.

Why carers ceased to foster

We now turn to the more vital question of why these former carers gave up fostering. Table 14.2 presents side by side the primary explanations offered by the surveyed former foster carers and those given by fostering staff/social work records.

Table 14.2

Why carers ceased to foster based on the views of former carers and fostering workers /records

Explanations	Former F/carers' Primary reason		Fostering workers' Primary reason	
	N	%	N	%
Dissatisfaction with the service	25	26	3	2
Retirement or illness	18	19	32	22
Adopted the foster child	17	18	19	13
Children's behaviour	16	17	8	5
Needing to work, move, no space	14	15	30	20
Impact on own family, no privacy	12	12	13	9
Stress, no respite	10	10	6	4
Allegations	5	5	17	11
At own request or had enough	–	–	12	8
Biological parents' behaviours	4	4	–	–
End of unique placement	2	2	4	3
Other (bereavement, no placements)	5	5	5	3
Total	**128***		**149**	

*The percentages are based on the number of carers and staff and because of multiple responses do not add up to 100.

While the main reasons for which foster carers cease to foster are diverse, there are also a number of consistent patterns which can be grouped into two broad categories: (i) internal factors connected with the fostering services; and (ii) external factors.

i) Internal factors connected with the operation of the fostering services included
- outright dissatisfaction with the operation of the fostering services;
- the children's behaviours;
- impact of fostering on own family/no privacy;
- burn-out/stress/no respite;
- allegations; and
- birth parents' behaviours.

The above areas of dissatisfaction amounted to 57 per cent of all the responses. If we were to add those who said they had left because of ill-health resulting from the stress of fostering, then around three-fifths of carers left because of some aspect connected with the operation of the fostering services. These reasons did not always have to do with the behaviour or attitudes of social workers or the agency. A large part of it was related to the general implications arising from caring for some very problematic children. There was no evidence to suggest that those who ceased were fostering more problematic children compared to the rest. Hardly any black, Asian or mixed parentage children also featured in the study. The Portsmouth study too found that about half the responses of those who ceased were in some way connected with the operation of the fostering services (Jones, 1975), albeit withdrawals were much higher in that study.

ii) External factors included
- the adoption of the foster child;
- no space or needing to work;
- illness/retirement; and
- moving house.

Adoption
With one exception, the 17 carers (or 18 per cent) who withdrew after adopting the foster child were amongst those most satisfied with the fostering services.

Illness and retirement

Over a fifth of former carers stopped either because of retirement, death of a partner, or poor health. In the case of the small number of former carers who said they gave up on account of ill health, it was not always possible to distinguish between illness that was stress induced as a result of the fostering task and illness that was unconnected with it. Both appeared to have played a part in a few cases. Although the great majority of women (82 per cent) said that their health had remained the same before and after stopping to foster, 13 per cent said that it had improved with only two per cent saying that it had deteriorated.

Moving house or needing to work

Moving house and/or needing to work accounted for around one in ten withdrawals. While two of these carers went on to foster in another authority, there was no evidence of the rest doing so. In fact only an insignificant proportion of existing carers said that, in the event of moving house, they would continue to foster in another area. The same proportion of former, as current, female carers were working outside the home, but former ones were far more likely to be doing so full rather than part-time after ceasing to foster.

Annual loss

Overall, the fostering services in Scotland can expect to have an annual loss of around seven per cent (between 80 and 100 carers) who leave because of dissatisfaction with fostering including the children's problems. If these figures were applied to England, it would result in around a thousand carers being lost each year. Waterhouse's (1997) study suggests an annual loss of around eight per cent in England.

Levels of congruence found between former carers and fostering workers/records

Though there were a number of similarities in the explanations offered by former carers and social workers of why carers ceased to foster, there were also significant differences. Fostering workers significantly underestimated the proportion of carers who withdrew because of dissatisfaction with the fostering services, the foster children's behaviours, stress and parental interference. They "exaggerated" the numbers of those who left because of moving house and/or the need to work, illness or retirement and 'own request'.

The most glaring difference between the two groups was the much higher proportion of carers to fostering workers, who said they had left fostering because of outright dissatisfaction with the operation of the fostering services (26 to 2 per cent). It could be argued that those who returned the postal questionnaire, or spoke to us, were not a true representation of all those who ceased to foster and that the fostering workers' views were more representative. We tried to check this by comparing the level of congruence in relation to individual cases (where we had the names) between the views expressed by social workers and those of former foster carers. Where foster carers gave as their main reason for withdrawing the 'lack of social work support', the 'attitudes and behaviour of social workers' or 'the activities of the social work department', fostering workers tended to say the carers had withdrawn 'at their own request', 'own decision' or that 'they had had enough', or 'because of work commitments'.

It seems that, in part, carers' real reasons for ceasing to foster were not conveyed to fostering staff or adequately recorded. In other instances, social work records used generalised explanations like 'own request' and 'own decision' which obscured the problem.

Comparisons of former and continuing carers

We can also make some comparisons between the explanations offered by the former carers who gave up because of factors associated with fostering, and those offered by continuing ones when describing times they felt like giving up. There were many similarities between the two. Both spoke about children's problems, chronic lack of social work support and related issues concerning the operation of the fostering service, including stress and effect on own family. On the basis of these findings, the difference between the two groups was one of degree rather than of substance. Eventually the pressure or a crisis becomes too much for some individuals tilting the balance towards withdrawal.

Working relationships with the fostering services

Next we contrasted the perceptions of former foster carers with those of current ones on the quality of relationships with the children's social workers, link workers, and the agency as a whole. The ratings of satisfaction offered by the former carers were, as expected, below those of current ones. The same applied when it came to the levels of support and whether expectations had been met or not.

However, it was thought that, to obtain a truer picture, all those carers who gave up for external reasons should be excluded from the analysis and it should concentrate instead on the 50 carers who left because of definite dissatisfaction with some key aspect of the operation of the fostering services. These form the basis for the next section.

Table 14.3

Contrasting the rating of relationships between current and former carers who left because of dissatisfaction with some aspect of the fostering service

Relationship level	Relationship with social workers		Relationship with link worker		Relationship with agency	
	Current	Former	Current	Former	Current	Former
Level	%	%	%	%	%	%
Very good	46	31	68	40	37	18
Good	32	22	22	31	45	36
Neither good nor bad	13	14	8	20	13	26
Poor	6	18	1	7	4	12
Very poor	3	14	1	2	1	8
Total	**100**	**99**	**100**	**100**	**100**	**100**

The overall picture that emerges from Table 14.3 is that just over half the former carers rated their relationship with the social workers and the agency as 'good' or 'very good', but the rating for 'very good' was notably lower. Compared to current carers, former carers rated all three types of relationships significantly lower. Perhaps it was to be expected that, as far as relationships were concerned, former carers would feel more disillusioned, compared to current ones.

Much of the dissatisfaction of the former carers with the children's social workers centred on the latter's failure to visit often enough; failure to provide sufficient background information on the child; being unresponsive to requests for help and support when the children were being difficult; being unappreciative of their efforts and not being available when needed. Typical comments included 'no support from child's social worker'; 'could have done with more support'; 'lack of commitment from certain social workers' or 'poor matching'.

Worse, in the eyes of the former carers, were telephone calls or other messages never being returned or being told the social worker was always somewhere else and unable to come to the phone: 'calls to child's social worker not being returned', 'no say in what happens' or 'being left to cope on our own'.

There were a variety of other comments suggesting that as carers they had had very little say in what happened to the children and there was little recognition of them as members of a working team or as partners.

Support

Another comparison made between the two groups of former and current carers was in the amount of support received.

Table 14.4
Levels of support as perceived by current and former carers

Level	Current %	Former %
Very good	37	12
Good	35	20
Neutral	18	40
Poor	7	16
Very poor	3	10
Total	**100**	**98**

The pattern found with relationships was repeated here but more strongly. Significantly fewer former, than current, carers described the level of support as 'very good' or 'good'. Correspondingly more former carers described support as neutral ('half and half') or as 'very poor' to 'poor'. Former carers repeated some of the comments made earlier, especially about infrequent visits, unavailability and unresponsiveness to requests for help. Nevertheless, many were satisfied with the support, but still gave up.

When asked to say whether their overall expectations of fostering had been met, only 29 per cent of those who gave up because of dissatisfaction with the fostering services said that they had. This contrasted with just over half of current carers who said their expectations were fulfilled. The main explanation for the apparent disappointment was of fostering turning out to be much harder than they had expected and the lack of support from the fostering services.

Fostering experience
We also compared former and current carers' characteristics and views on the service, in relation to their length of service. Carers who ceased to foster had an average of 7.5 years of fostering experience compared to 7.0 years of continuing ones. Even taking account of only those who ceased because of dissatisfaction with some aspect of the work of the fostering services, their fostering experience still amounted to an average of 7.3 years. It cannot be said, therefore, that those who withdraw generally do so only after a short period of caring. Just under half had fostered for less than five years, but over a quarter had fostered for more than ten years (see Table 14.5). In fact, only nine per cent had fostered for less than a year compared to 40 per cent found by Jones (1975). However, almost all those who gave up before the first year was over were those who were dissatisfied with the fostering service.

The large percentage of carers leaving after a year prompted Jones (1975) to write that 'there is little to be gained from higher recruitment of foster parents if large numbers or recruits cease to foster after only a short period as an active foster parent' (p 41). There is no answer, perhaps, to the question of how long carers should be expected to foster before they give up. Would the perception of themselves as doing a professional job or having a career make any difference, or does the demanding nature of the job impose its own time limits? Carers on the whole do not see themselves as making a career out of fostering.

Table 14.5
The number of years former carers had fostered compared with current carers

No. of Years	Former carers		Current carers	
	N	*%*	*N*	*%*
0–5	15	48	418	52
6–10	25	26	179	22
11–20	23	24	170	21
21–30	2	2	34	4
30 +	–	–	5	1
Total	**95***	**100**	**806**	**100**

* *One missing*

The factors that triggered the final decision

Apart from those who retired or stopped fostering because of other external factors, the decision by the rest of the carers to cease fostering was not usually taken lightly. In the view of many, the situation had been building up over a period of time, but the final decision was usually triggered by some recent event such as: action or inaction by the social work services; the behaviour of the placed child; deterioration of their own health; the need for a break; or the end of a placement. Typical comments illustrating the precipitating factor included 'disillusionment with the social work department'; 'trying to argue with social workers for better matching'; 'lack of support'; 'child's bad behaviour increased'; 'the end of the placement seemed a good time' or 'we could not take any more – our health and our family's life were affected'.

While the majority said that once they decided to stop, nothing would have made them change their minds, there were a few who indicated that changes in attitudes within the social work services might have stopped them from giving up. Typical comments included: 'with more support'; 'if the social work department's attitudes were different'; or 'changes in the social work department'.

Some of the above comments were repeated when asked what, if anything, might bring them back to fostering. A number mentioned changes in the operation of the fostering services, more space in their house, better health, better pay and better conditions of service or after their adopted child settled down. The total numbers of possible returnees, assuming their grievances were attended to, did not amount, however, to more than 10 per cent of all those who ceased to foster within a year.

SUMMARY

- The annual actual loss of foster carers for all reasons in both Scotland and England are less than 10 per cent. Former carers in Scotland fostered for an average of 7.5 years and so had made a significant contribution before stopping. Some authorities in the sample demonstrated that they could keep their carers longer.
- There was no evidence that the majority of foster carers gave up easily. The reasons why they withdrew were diverse, but almost three-fifths were related to some aspect connected with the operation of the fostering service, including the children's problems, and the rest to external factors.
- Background characteristics and declared motivation, in most respects, were similar to those of current carers. The eventual decision to cease fostering by those who were dissatisfied is a culmination of four main interacting factors:
  - a past history of unresponsiveness and unavailability of social work support;
  - the child being more difficult than expected;
  - unresponsiveness to requests for help and support during the most recent crisis; and
  - impact on own family.
- The lower than expected losses should not lead to complacency. Many of the dissatisfactions expressed by those who ceased to foster were also shared by a significant proportion of continuing foster carers and require urgent attention. They include the lack of support and general

social work and management attitudes, the impact of fostering on their families, and stress. The main reason why they do not give up is their commitment to the child and their awareness of child care need.

15 Financial arrangements

This chapter sets out the financial arrangements made by local authorities in relation to their foster carers. It also covers payment schemes, allowances, individual grants and insurance. These arrangements are discussed in the light of the carers' expectations and observations.

BACKGROUND

Foster carers enter into contractual agreements to deliver fostering services without being treated as employees of the authorities. For their efforts they are paid an allowance for each child's upkeep and the authorities also take responsibility for all the other expenses associated with looking after a child or young person. In many cases a reward element is either built into the allowance or paid as an extra in the form of a fee. Two-fifths of all carers in our survey were in receipt of such a fee.

Over the years, debate and controversy have focused on levels of allowances; additional expenses involved; matters of insurance; whether carers should be rewarded for their efforts; and the efficiency of the machinery set up to make the payments.

FINANCIAL ISSUES

Reference was made in Chapter 1 to other studies linking higher allowances to better recruitment and better retention of carers (Simon, 1975; Campbell and Whitelaw-Downs, 1987; Chamberlain et al, 1992). Previous studies and publications have also highlighted the great disparities in payments between authorities across Britain to the confusion and sometimes frustration of carers. Besides such disparities are the different schemes operated by different authorities. As a result, significant differences can exist both between neighbouring authorities and within authorities for caring for similar children (Bebbington and Miles 1990; Lowe, 1990; Pithouse et al, 1994; Waterhouse, 1997; Oldfield, 1997).

Attitudes in favour of the non-payment of carers have developed over many decades, viewing caring as an act of total altruism and a sign of unselfishness, being done 'for love not money'. Such expectations appear to persist since, as stated in Chapter 4, very few carers mentioned finance as a motivating factor, even though a substantial proportion (20 per cent) of male carers were not working. Based on her study, Rhodes (1993) remarked that 'foster care now teeters uneasily between the traditional charitable model and the alternative model of a professional salaried service' (p 9).

Some carers were concerned that, if this study were to highlight their commitment to the children, it might be used as an excuse for denying them better conditions of service. Their fears were not unjustified. As recently as 1998, the House of Commons Health Committee was told by the Parliamentary Under-Secretary that fostering 'would be in danger of ceasing to be a vocation if there were to be an element of reward in payments to foster carers' (p 35). The Committee did not accept this argument.

PAYMENT SCHEMES

This study identified four main payment schemes existing side by side within authorities, with most operating more than one and sometimes three or four schemes at the same time (see Table 15.1). The main schemes identified were basic allowances; enhanced allowances; fees; basic allowances plus a fee for some.

Table 15.1
The authorities' schemes for paying foster carers

Scheme	%
Only basic allowances for all	6
Basic plus enhanced allowances for some	78
Basic allowances plus a fee for all	25
Basic allowances plus a fee for some	34

Only six per cent of authorities paid their foster carers the basic maintenance allowance without any additional enhancement allowances or fees. Besides the basic allowance, the great majority of authorities (78 per cent) paid some carers a discretionary enhanced allowance which depended on the assessed needs of the child. Enhanced allowances were mainly paid to carers fostering adolescents and teenagers, children with a disability, or those of any age group with serious emotional/behavioural problems. Some authorities also automatically paid enhancements for sibling groups. Enhancements could amount to anything up to 100 per cent on the top of the basic allowance.

A quarter of all authorities paid a fee to all their carers in addition to the basic child allowance. In the majority of these authorities, the fee increased with the age of the child. A third of the authorities paid an additional fee, but only to selected groups of carers, mainly those fostering for a special scheme involving the fostering of adolescents or children with disabilities. Finally, in exceptional circumstances, such as in the case of a child with multiple disabilities, authorities could pay four types of allowances/fees, that is: a maintenance allowance, an enhanced maintenance allowance, a fee, and an enhanced fee.

The practice of some authorities to pay fees or enhanced allowances selectively has created tensions among carers (see also Shaw and Hipgrave, 1989). In view also of the different payment schemes run and the multiplicity of schemes operating even within a single agency, it was perhaps not surprising to find that some carers felt confused about the whole system and sometimes angry about the disparities. It appeared sometimes accidental whether or not a carer was paid only a basic maintenance allowance, a fee or an enhanced allowance. This could largely depend on the route followed for accommodating, especially adolescents, or the kind of grouping an adolescent was assigned to e.g. 'temporary', 'long term', 'planned' or 'unplanned', or whether a carer already belonged to a scheme or not. Some carers also criticised the age differentials of fee-paying schemes when, it was claimed, equally diffi- cult and problematic children could be found in any age group.

Basic maintenance allowances
Levels of fostering maintenance allowances in Britain were first intro- duced almost one and a half centuries ago by the Poor Law authorities. The allowances were meant to cover the additional costs to a family of

looking after a child placed with them. Boarding-out regulations encouraged carers to look after the foster child as if it were their own, thereby implying the maintenance of the same standards of care and standard of living (for more details see Oldfield, 1997).

The costs of maintaining a child in foster care have often been a matter of controversy. Debates have concerned what to include, what to compare it with, and whether the allowance should keep up with the rise in prices. Furthermore, Oldfield (1997) demonstrated in her detailed analysis of household expenditures that foster children incur greater costs than other children and concluded that there was evidence of a shortfall in the foster care allowances to meet the aggregate direct costs of maintaining the foster child. This applied to all ages of foster children but especially for children under the age of 11 years.

For a number of years now, the National Foster Care Association (NFCA) has published its own annual minimum recommended allowances which local authorities have been expected to follow in their payments to carers. The minimum is calculated on the age related official Family Expenditure Survey and Equivalence Income Scales which are published each year. The allowance is meant to cover such items as housing, food, fuel, clothing, household goods, household services, personal care, ordinary fares and leisure activities. The minimum maintenance weekly allowances set by NFCA for 1996/97 were:

Age Group

0–4	5–10	11–15	16+
£54.18	£67.20	£83.63	£108.36

By 1997, almost all Scottish authorities were paying the recommended NFCA scales with only insignificant variations of above and below payments. Much wider variations, though, were found in England with some carers receiving four times the basic rate offered to others (NFCA, 1997; Waterhouse, 1997).

Enhanced allowances and fees

The idea of rewarding foster carers, because of the special needs of the child, is a relatively new one having been introduced in the last quarter of the 20th century. It was a decisive shift away from viewing fostering as a totally altruistic and voluntary activity with no expectation of reward, to that of a professional activity similar to a job. It was also a recognition of the changing nature of fostering from caring for mostly unproblematic children to those with often serious emotional and behavioural difficulties or those who had some kind of disability. As we shall see later, carers themselves would like to be rewarded for their efforts, even though not many yet treated fostering as a career.

Within authorities payments for foster carers come in the form of enhanced allowances or fees and exceptionally both. We recognise that some authorities look upon an enhanced allowance as something between a reward and a compensation for increased costs to carers, but it was difficult for the study to pursue the different interpretations given to the concept of "enhanced allowances". Calculating payments or rewards for the care of a child and the extra time involved in such matters as general care, the general household activities of cleaning, laundry, repairing, "treatment" care, administration, travel, time for visits to schools and doctors or to attend review meetings, is a complex process.

Why some authorities developed fee paying schemes and others preferred to reward carers through enhanced allowances depended on an agency's perception of the role and tasks of foster carers with practicalities concerning resources and the carers' economic circumstances particularly in relation to income tax and benefits.

The tax position of carers was reported to have largely influenced the policy for enhanced allowances pursued in the West of Scotland, though the tax position appears to be that any sum over and above "expenses" becomes taxable income and affects benefits. There was also the view that discretionary enhancement would allow for a more equitable distribution of resources based on a case by case assessment. From accounts given to the study, enhancement and discretion seem to have led to more problems about inequities than the payment of fees. We were told that some of the new authorities in this part of the country were now considering replacing enhanced allowances with fees.

The payment of fees

The following types of fee payment were identified:

- fees paid to all carers with the value of the fee depending on the child's age (seven authorities);
- flat fees for all carers (one agency);
- fees to all with the value depending on levels of skills/training (one agency).
- fees paid only to those fostering for special schemes (11 authorities).

The weekly fees paid for 1997/98 by one authority in Scotland varied by age group as follows:

	Age Group	
0–8	*9–11*	*12–18*
£34.05	£52.40	£107.85

Other authorities who had adopted the comprehensive fee system were paying broadly similar amounts. Several authorities were selectively paying fees only to those of their carers who fostered for a community care scheme, that is, looking after adolescents/teenagers. One authority paid a flat fee of £112 per week to all its carers, but this was reduced for second and subsequent children. Another paid a salary to a carer to look after a single child with multiple disabilities and special needs. If successful, the agency planned to extend it. Local authority fees were approximately a third of those paid by the emerging non-statutory sector which was recruiting carers mainly to take adolescents.

The payment of fees to all carers did not appear to influence overall carer numbers in each agency, but as already said elsewhere, those carers who were paid a fee were more satisfied than others with the delivery of the fostering services, more likely to attend training sessions and support groups and to recognise that there were benefits for children seeing their parents. Though it is recognised that the numbers are small, nevertheless, of the seven authorities that paid all their carers a fee, only one was experiencing "serious" placement shortages. A caution, however, is necessary. Though it would be interesting to think that the payment of fees was the decisive factor, with one exception all the authorities that paid fees to all their carers were in semi-rural or rural areas. It has been pointed out elsewhere in this book that far more carers per household in Scotland came from rural than urban areas. This means that geographical location may be more important than the payment of fees as far as recruitment is concerned.

Further evidence that the connection between fees and "no serious shortages" was possibly spurious came from another source. This study contrasted those authorities that paid a fee with those that paid enhancement, less than 50 per cent enhancements, or fees paid only to selected groups of carers. In this case there were no differences between the authorities as far as levels of recruitment and loss of carers were concerned. In contrast to our findings, the NFCA study found that authorities paying at the lower end of their seven point scale 'were over-represented in rarely offering a placement choice to children of all ages' (Waterhouse, 1997, p 67).

The payment of enhanced allowances
Authorities were asked to indicate the approximate percentage of total placements attracting more than their basic rate of fostering allowance as defined by the NFCA. In both Scotland and England, only a tiny number of authorities indicated that they paid none of their carers an enhanced allowance. In contrast, almost half paid over 50 per cent over the NFCA recommended basic rate.

Almost a third of the authorities in Scotland and two-fifths in England had set no maximum financial limit in relation to individual placements but the rest did so. Two-thirds of the authorities in Scotland and almost nine out of ten in England had also set no payment limits so far for using a foster placement provided by another agency (Waterhouse, 1997). This policy could change, we were told, in the light of the kind of placement fees the non-statutory sector was beginning to charge authorities.

SINGLE GRANTS

Single grants are given to carers to help meet additional expenses on behalf of the children in the form of clothing, footwear, holidays, transport, special classes and so on. Some authorities pay an extra weekly sum on top of the minimum allowance to cover some of these items such as clothing and footwear, but there are many other additional expenses that cannot satisfactorily be included into the minimum allowance and have to be negotiated separately. Official guidance and hand-outs create an expectation that social workers will take the initiative to ask for grants, but this was not the case in practice. Worse, as stated earlier, was the reported stereotype that a minority of social workers felt that foster carers were always asking for special grants.

A majority of authorities said that they operated a 'well defined' policy on individual grants mainly in relation to telephones, transport and school meals, meaning that those who met the criteria were automatically entitled to the grant. For all the other items the majority exercised discretion. Mostly the child's social worker, and occasionally link workers, were seen as responsible for submitting applications on behalf of carers for additional grants. Some of the delays in the payment of grants were attributed to staff failing to complete and submit to the finance office the necessary forms required for payment.

There were variations between authorities as to who finally decided the award of individual grants to carers. Most applications were considered by the service manager, sometimes by the team manager, and on occasions by a deputy director or even a chief social work officer. In some authorities, and depending on the amount involved, all these tiers of management would be involved in approving a single grant, making the process protracted. Some processes felt off-putting to staff who had to prepare and process an application and to the carers initiating it. Sellick (1992) found from his study of carers who joined the independent sector that one of the motivating factors for doing so was to avoid the many arguments over additional grants.

Insurance cover for carers

Foster carers raised a number of issues concerning insurance for themselves and the child. The main one was to be covered by the agency for damages caused to their home and outside by a foster child and for themselves to be covered for their legal liabilities as foster carers or for injuries suffered, such as an attack by a young person.

Disputes between carers and authorities over malicious or accidental damage caused by foster children or arising from the theft of carers' property were not frequent, but when they occurred they could lead to ill feeling and a sense of unfairness. The question of who paid for what was complex and far from clear. For example, compensation claims for damage to property caused by a young foster person would sometimes be judged on whether a carer said something that might have provoked the young person.

The most widely available insurance cover, provided by half the authorities on behalf of their carers, was for public liability. After that the number of authorities who provided insurance cover for a range of possibilities varied between a sixth and a third. Some of the remaining authorities were considering either introducing insurance cover, or dealing with the matter differently. For example, several authorities had taken out an NFCA membership insurance cover, others encouraged carers to take out their own and either paid for it or enhanced the basic allowance to cover it. Several others had their own compensation scheme to which carers were expected to apply.

The variety of schemes available and the complexities surrounding them explain, perhaps, some of the difficulties and the kind of disputes carers claimed to have had when trying to make claims. Authorities were equally wary about some of the claims made and the escalating costs, making it even more necessary, in the view of several managers, for an arbitration system to be in place.

The carers' perspective

Over 800 active carers who participated in the study answered questions and made comments on a range of financial issues concerned with levels of payment, single grants and methods of payment.

Levels of payment

Around two out of five carers thought that the present levels of payments were about right, with only a few (four per cent) saying that they were generous. On the other hand, almost three in five described them as on the low side (see Table 15.2). The age and experience of carers did not affect the rating.

No consistent pattern has emerged from the responses of carers from different authorities with different payment schemes. For example, in one agency, where all carers were paid a fee, three-quarters said the level of payment was on the low side. This contrasted with three-fifths who said this in the total sample and 45 per cent in another large agency, where only allowances and enhanced allowances were paid and where the level of unemployment among carers was higher. Yet again, in another agency where only enhanced allowances rather than fees were operating, 87 per cent said that payment was on the low side.

A series of other questions were asked concerning allowances and fees and the answers are summarised in Table 15.2.

Table 15.2
Foster carers, authorities and payments

	Agree strongly		Agree		50/50		Disagree strongly		Disagree		Total
	N	%	N	%	N	%	N	%	N	%	%
1. Fostering is a job and should be salaried appropriately											
	278	35	206	26	191	24	74	9	46	6	100
2. Without fostering fees we would not be able to continue fostering											
	289	39	192	27	127	17	99	14	24	3	100
3. It is always difficult to ask social workers for special grants											
	136	18	180	23	184	24	229	29	47	6	100
4. Carers are not always told about extra allowances											
	272	34	261	33	126	16	109	14	23	3	100
5. Payment is often delayed											
	187	24	232	30	161	21	166	21	27	4	100

Should fostering be seen as a job?

Whether fostering should be seen as a job and be salaried accordingly received outright support by around three in five carers with only 15 per cent being opposed to it. Those already being paid a fee, most of whom were also fostering for the community care schemes, were more likely than the rest to support the idea of a salary. The small percentage of carers who disagreed that the allowance was not enough, or that the service should be salaried, stressed the enjoyment they got out of fostering, the thought of offering a service to children, or disliking the idea of 'making money' out of fostering.

> *I enjoy it, so it cannot be a job. If you are paid, you are not really being a parent to them. It makes it easier to look after them when not paid for doing it.*

Those who supported the idea put forward mainly financial arguments, though some also stressed that a salaried or part-salaried service would be much more attractive to newcomers and be an incentive to continue fostering. A salaried service, it was further argued, would safeguard pensions, holiday rights and sickness benefits and would also act as a kind of recognition for the demanding nature of the work. Even attaching pensions to fees as an interim measure would go some way to satisfy some carers and perhaps also attract others to fostering. Some carers gave the example of fostering two to three children at a time for over 15 years and then having to rely solely on the state pension. 'Somehow,' as one said, 'it is not right'.

In interviews, most carers drew parallels with others in the care sector whose work was properly paid without questioning their motives or whether 'it would attract the wrong kind':

> *Foster carers are not properly salaried, recognised or valued and yet it is unrivalled as it involves a commitment of the whole family.*

A number of carers, who were also child minding, were considering moving to full-time child minding as they found it better paid and much less demanding.

One drawback identified with the payments of a salary or fees was the position of those who are now on benefits or on income support. It was argued that the payment of either fees or salaries, as opposed to enhanced allowances, would have to be high enough to justify the loss of social security benefits or the payment of tax. Failing this, it could result in the loss of income to some carers who need it badly.

The vital importance of fees

Like the idea of a salaried service, those already paid a fee and those fostering for community care schemes were more likely than the rest to say that they could not manage without a fee. The two-thirds who agreed that without a fee they would not be able to continue fostering, did not mean that they were going to give up fostering soon. They mainly wanted to make the point that fostering was underpaid and undervalued. As Ramsay (1996) also points out from a study in Fife, the professional fee reduces the need for people to find alternative paid employment, as some did. We were given examples of how some carers had to rely on private means or on a partner's outside salary or on their combined wages to manage.

> ... no hardship because enough money from other sources and our joint wages.

Those who opposed the idea of a salary were also likely to disagree with the statement that, without a fee, they would be unable to continue.

Special grants

Two-fifths of carers agreed with the statement that it was difficult to ask social workers for special grants, with over a third definitely disagreeing and the rest (24 per cent) being uncertain. There was a clear association between overall dissatisfaction with the child's social worker and finding it difficult to ask for a grant. Besides allowances and fees, the two-fifths who agreed said that money was like 'a taboo subject', rarely raised or discussed at meetings or during visits. They had in mind single payments for such items as clothing, footwear, transport, telephones, holidays and insurance. The point these carers wanted to make was that it should be the responsibility of the agency to raise and discuss such issues rather than waiting for carers to do so:

> It feels mean to be asking for money.

Being reluctant to ask for single payments tied in closely with the next statement which was that 'Carers are not always told about extra allowances'. Over two-thirds of the carers agreed with the statement. In comments many of them said that they did not always have enough information about what was available and whether it was a 'right' or 'discretionary'. Some authorities which had handbooks outlining the financial arrangements had either not updated them or not distributed them. Other carers found the handbooks not user friendly or lacking in detail. It was also claimed that some visiting staff were themselves unaware of what single payments were available and what carers were entitled to claim for:

> When I started fostering, very little information was given about money and especially about any extras and special payments. I asked for a booklet but none was available.

Some carers made reference to the embarrassment, hesitations, and sometimes 'humiliation' they felt when having to ask for single grants:

> I had to grovel to get extras. Instead of them asking, I was the one always begging.

A lot of bad feeling and sometimes 'resentment' was generated because of lack of clear rules or disputes over compensation for damages, holidays, transport or equipment. A number of carers said that they were 'subsidising' the local authority in the day to day care of the children. Carers also expected time to be taken during group and individual meetings to explain entitlements to allowances, fees, individual grants and to any additional financial assistance that was available. It was also important to them that they knew which grants were discretionary and how they were assessed and which ones were an entitlement.

Sellick's (1992) interviews with carers who joined the independent sector showed that one of the main reasons was to avoid the continued arguments over additional grants. Respondents to this study indicated that they would consider joining another fostering agency provided that not only was the pay right but that they were convinced that the support provided to the children and themselves was satisfactory.

Payment is often delayed

Over half the carers agreed or strongly agreed that payments, especially of grants, were delayed, sometimes for very long periods. Only a quarter indicated that their authorities were very efficient in the way payments arrived. In some authorities, over 70 per cent of carers agreed or strongly agreed that payment was often delayed, in contrast to others where it was down to 32 per cent. Some carers who were owed around £1,000 had to wait months before being paid. Those on benefits or on weekly wages found delays more frustrating:

> . . . *waiting for up to a year and a half for money owed.*

Berridge (1997) attributes the general "inefficiency" in the payment of foster carers to the "low" position they occupy in the organisation.

The mismanagement of the carers' financial interests reflected not only the efficiency or otherwise of the finance department, but also of the child's social worker. Some carers claimed that some staff failed to ensure that the necessary forms were prepared and forwarded to the Finance Section in time for payment. Not surprising, perhaps, dissatisfaction with delays also overlapped with dissatisfaction with the activities of the child's social worker. This also explained the differences we found between different districts within the same authority.

THE AGENCIES' RESPONSE TO THE CARERS' ASPIRATIONS

This part of the study concluded that, even leaving aside levels of pay, there was still considerable dissatisfaction among carers about the financial arrangements. This was unrelated to the carers' age, status or length of fostering experience, except that carers in receipt of a fee were more likely to support the idea of a salaried service and to feel more satisfied with the delivery of the fostering services. Based on the carers' comments, four major financial issues stood out that required urgent attention:

- levels and uniformity of payments;
- policies and practices about single grants;
- efficiency with payments;
- clarity about entitlements.

Within the present climate of budgetary limitations, no new policies were emerging within local authorities that would take account of the majority of carers' aspirations for better reward and improved financial conditions of service. The most authorities were determined to do was to improve their methods of payment and clarify their written policies in relation to single grants and insurance. A few others were contemplating the introduction of fees to replace enhanced allowances. In addition, some of the authorities who have been paying fees, with the value of the fee depending on the child's age, have been considering abolishing the age tiers as a recognition that most children in foster care now present a challenge to their carers. Such a step, it was claimed, would also move away from labelling children as "problems" before their carers were paid a fee. One other authority adopted the first scheme of its kind in Scotland to link the payment of fees to the carers' 'skills and training'. This came into effect on 1 April 1998. While many managers we spoke to would welcome a national scheme that identified career paths for carers, they also stressed the complex operational problems surrounding it.

SUMMARY

- Almost all the authorities had standardised the basic fostering allowance paid to carers based on the NFCA's annually recommended figures, which are in turn based on the government's Family Expenditure Survey.
- The study found a multiplicity of payment schemes. Which carers were rewarded and why lacked clarity, consistency or fairness.
- Fees and/or enhanced allowances were paid to foster carers by most authorities as a form of reward. Payments made by the non-statutory sector were said to be three or more times higher than those paid by local authorities.
- Carers who were paid a fee were more satisfied than the rest with the operation of the fostering services, more likely to attend training and support group meetings, and to see benefits for the children seeing their parents. This could be attributed to the possibility that they were also receiving more support and attention than other carers.

- The majority of individual grants given to carers were discretionary and were mostly decided by service managers. Procedures for claims were complex, unclear and rather off-putting.
- The study established the following financial concerns on the part of carers:

  levels and uniformity of payments; policies and practices about individual grants; efficiency with payments; clarity about entitlements.

- The majority of carers, irrespective of age, status and years of experience, found the present levels of allowances/pay low and were also in support of a salaried or part-salaried service. Those who did not support the idea of a salaried service overlapped with many of those who did not attend training or support groups.
- Within a climate of serious budgetary restraints, little evidence was found to suggest that authorities were moving towards responding to the financial expectations and aspirations of their carers. There was more optimism concerning greater efficiency in the payment of carers.

16 Conclusions and overview

INTRODUCTION

We have reported here the findings of a study which looked at the delivery of foster care from the perspective of foster carers and local authority fostering agencies. The study was prompted mainly by concerns to do with the perceived inadequate supply of foster carers and with issues of recruitment and retention. Though the study was set up in Scotland, similar concerns were voiced in England.

The main task faced by the study was to establish the extent of the shortages, where these occurred, and to which type of need they applied most. Furthermore, it was necessary to obtain the carers' perspectives on the delivery of the service and identify how policy and organisational matters influenced such delivery, including the recruitment and retention of carers. In the process of doing so, four main sets of data were brought together:

- The views of current and former carers;
- the views of service and senior child care managers;
- agency documents;
- the results of the census survey.

In this final chapter we bring together the strengths and limitations of the fostering services and emerging themes from the study and their implications for policy makers, management, practice and national government. The main strengths of the Scottish and English fostering services as perceived by the authorities and identified by the foster carers in Scotland are outlined in the next two tables. Looking at these strengths, there is considerable overlap between the managers' and carers' views, especially around the commitment of carers, the specialist nature of the service, the support offered to carers by placement workers and the fee structure (where available). Though there are no similar previous studies to compare the findings with, what has emerged suggests that the fostering services are fairly consistent in the delivery of services. These strengths could account for the low losses of carers found.

Table 16:1
The strength of the fostering service

Authorities (Scotland)	Authorities (England)	Carers (Scotland)*
• Committed placement staff	• Skilled & dedicated staff	• The placement worker system
• Committed carers	• Experienced carers plus good partnership	• Preparation and training
• The quality of support offered by placement staff	• Good recruitment, assessment, training & support services	• The fee paying structure (where available)
• The specialist nature of the placement service	• Independent placement service	• Group meetings/ support
• The fee structure (where available)	• Good management & commitment by agency	• Good recruitment, assessment, training & support services
• The greater integration of the fostering and residential services	• Generous/flexible financial systems	
• Of children placed, six in ten went to first choice placements	• Clear procedures and standards	

* We do not have the views of carers in England.

When it came to the service's difficulties, there was very little difference between the authorities' view in Scotland and England but there were significant differences between these and the carers' views.

217

In spite of the many strengths identified, major gaps and limitations also remain. These impact, among other things, on issues of recruitment, retention and direct service delivery. For example, significant associations were found, on the one hand, between levels of carer satisfaction with certain aspects closely connected with the operation of the fostering services, with the role and activities of the child's social worker and the agency as a whole and, on the other, with prematurely ceasing to foster, finding the children more difficult, and expectations of fostering not being met. All the key themes as well as those outlined below have also been given a big profile in the recently published UK National Standards for Foster Care (NFCA, 1999).

Table 16.2
The main difficulties of the fostering service

Scotland (agency view)	England (agency view)	Carers' view (Scotland)
• Not enough social worker time	• Financial deficiencies	• Poor availability of child's social worker
• Shortage of foster carers	• Shortages of foster carers	• Inadequate support
• Budgetary constraints	• Poor sensitivity to placement issues	• The children's problems
• Some carers' attitude to training	• Staffing deficiencies	• Not valuing or listening by agency
• Tensions between placement workers and children's social workers	• Poor communication between placement workers and fieldworkers	• Insufficient information on children
• Lack of policy direction	• Scattered/diverse/ inconsistent service	• No team work
• Low pay for carers		• Low pay and poor financial practices
		• Fears about allegations of abuse

* *Waterhouse (1997).*

Structures and organisation

While some councils and managers were still searching for the "best possible" structure for the fostering service, in other areas change was prompted mainly by budgetary constraints. Yet reducing manpower, without sufficient safeguards, could accentuate further some of the service delivery problems found by the study or undermine some of the achievements of the service. The study found that separate foster care units had some advantages over area team attachments, but there are other factors that each agency has to consider before deciding the structure of its fostering service. These include the size of an agency; geographical factors; the expertise available; the management and degree of co-operation between staff; and how the activities of the placement staff can be ring-fenced and protected.

A highly regarded asset of the service was its placement worker system which operated consistently across Scotland and was available to most foster carers. The distinctiveness of the placement part of the service, whether operating from single units, district units or based in area teams, combined organisational coherence with considerable expertise. It is this distinctiveness that in our view has proved to be the backbone of the service, eliciting high praise from carers.

Possibly because of this distinctiveness and of accumulated expertise, this branch of the service has wrongly come to be known as 'the fostering service' to the detriment of the other part of the work undertaken by children's social workers operating from within area teams. This kind of identification goes beyond semantics in that it has shaped the attitudes of some staff and carers as to whose responsibility it is to deliver the fostering services, and perhaps contributed to some of the tensions found within the service.

As the study has also found, these two branches of the fostering service, that is, the placement service and the child's social worker service, currently operate with very different degrees of effectiveness. Fostering knowledge and expertise were said to be most evident among placement staff and least amongst children's social workers and their immediate managers. The challenge is to bring the latter part of the service up to the same standard as that of the placement service or unify the two into a single fostering service.

More radically, in our view, the challenge is on policy makers and managers to gradually move towards the integration and unification of all their child placement services under a single management and service delivery system, without the loss of their distinctiveness. A highly knowledgeable, specialised and efficient service, untrammelled by other responsibilities such as child protection and emergencies, is required to engage in recruitment and respond to the needs of all looked after children, including the provision of direct support services to children and their carers. Integration is necessary at all levels, including management, with clear guidelines setting out who does what. This form of integration should also enable authorities to offer flexible packages to looked after children, their families and foster carers. Unlike now, a move in this direction should also empower managers to hold front line staff and carers more accountable for their activities.

In the meantime, much more could be achieved by greater emphasis being placed on better co-ordination and communication between social workers, placement workers, carers and their immediate managers. This requires senior management giving more guidance to lower management on how to prioritise their staff's time and how to manage staff with performance criteria in mind. Currently, both higher and lower management are also handicapped in being able to exercise a full monitoring role because of the absence of sophisticated management information technology systems.

Fostering policies and strategies

Since the late 1980s, foster care has become the principal "out-of-home" form of care for children looked after away from home, exceeding that of residential care. In spite of this, there are many signs that foster care does not yet have the high profile that was traditionally reserved for residential care within local authorities. Like their predecessors, a number of the new councils made general, rather than specific, policy statements with no long-term fostering strategic planning. Detail was mostly missing, including how objectives were meant to be achieved, the kind of resources to be made available, and the specific roles to be played by staff.

The official policy of wanting to keep as many children as possible in the community, including foster care, but without additional resourcing and detailed strategies and plans, places social work staff under considerable stress. The child's social workers, especially, do not have enough time to assess children, visit them and their carers more frequently, or to engage in much direct work with children. There was some dismay amongst many placement managers because too much emphasis was placed on child protection compared to the fostering service. The thrust of the policies which were emerging was mainly directed towards maintaining the status quo, and largely failed to take account of the many challenges currently facing the fostering service, including:

- the changing nature of fostering and the type of child now being fostered;
- the proportion of children requiring foster care who are not being placed;
- the gaps in existing services, especially the provision of support to children and carers;
- the rising aspirations of the great majority of foster carers;
- demographic changes and employment factors that influence recruitment;
- the emergence of a non-statutory fostering sector.

While budgetary constraints faced by all local authorities were partly responsible for this, evidence also suggested that the fostering service was still being perceived in some quarters as a semi-amateur kind of activity undertaken largely by volunteer carers who had a special commitment to children facing adversities in their lives. With a number of notable exceptions, there was a failure at the top level of management and within certain councils to recognise the evolution of fostering into a professional service demanding wide ranging skills and knowledge from those who deliver it, including carers. As a result, the profile of foster care found was rather low, the service in some authorities "marginalised" and not always commanding adequate attention within a climate of continued prioritising of resource allocation.

During the change-over from the regional to unitary authorities, many carers expressed concerns about the ability of the new authorities to properly resource the fostering service, drawing attention to their small budgets and the inexperience of some councillors and senior managers in the new councils as regards social work and fostering issues. Some of these concerns were later echoed by a number of child care and place-ment managers. Particularly, corporate type management structures, and those heading them, were felt to be too far removed from the aims and daily concerns of the service to understand its needs and resourcing.

Recruitment and retention

One positive finding from the study was that, during the year 1996/97, new carer recruitment exceeded losses by 46 per cent, which helped to bring up the number of all foster carers in Scotland to 2,203 or one carer for about every 938 households. Some evidence was also found suggest-ing that a few of the new smaller authorities were able to tap carer resources previously not reached by the larger regional authorities. The proportion of active carers, however, varies widely between different parts of the country, suggesting scope for much further improvement. The big cities, the central belt and the West of Scotland have most need for carers, but their recruitment levels were below average and in some areas well below.

If the recent recruitment rate is maintained, it could also signify an end to the gradual erosion of foster carer resources that has been happening since the late 1960s. Nevertheless, the majority of carers still decide to foster when it suits their family and personal circum-stances and, similarly, leave when these change. This knowledge presents a challenge to authorities to make fostering attractive enough to encourage carers to see fostering as a career and stay on for longer. As an example, some authorities were able to hold on to their carers for an average of up to ten years, compared to the overall average of seven years. Reaching an average of ten years reduces the need for new carers by about a third.

There can be no complacency, though, concerning both the low level of losses of carers and improvements in carer recruitment. More than half of those who leave the service do so mainly because of dissatisfac-tion with some aspect of its operation, including the children's behaviours. Furthermore, around half of active carers at any one time think of doing the same, with many of their complaints being similar to the ones held by those who give up.

One of the most potent recruitment methods found was by "word of mouth". This, however, works best if the message that is spread is a positive one. Only satisfied carers can recommend fostering to their relatives, friends, neighbours and to people at work. It is not accidental, perhaps, that the study found many carers clustered in the same streets, neighbourhoods or villages, yet elsewhere there were none. Taking the carers' comments on a number of related questions on the subject, recruitment messages would also have to address some key issues that carers consider hold back others from putting themselves forward to foster. They include:

- lack of awareness among the public about child care and fostering needs;
- fears of not measuring up to agency expectations and being rejected;
- lack of confidence about being able to do the job satisfactorily;
- the poor image of the children and the stereotype that children needing fostering are "bad";
- the "poor" image of social workers and the apparent credibility gap between them and the public, including their failure to deliver promised services.

To address these more specific factors, authorities have to project fostering as a longer term undertaking responding to career aspirations and as suiting both sexes. Furthermore, they need to show that the variety of children needing foster care could fit with the domestic arrangements of almost any household, including those of single people. It is also important to project:

- child care needs and the benefits of fostering to the children;
- an "honest" and balanced view of what fostering is about;
- the personal and financial rewards, including career prospects; and
- the availability of continued training and support.

As stated in Chapter 5, recruitment campaigns were mostly episodic and unsystematic, with no clear targets and lacking in clarity as to who to address, what issues to address, and how. The expectation of quick results clouded the views of some managers on the value of campaigns. Long-term strategies on recruitment were exceptional rather than the norm and foster carer recruitment did not permeate the whole agency, and sometimes not even its child care part. The urgency, in many authorities, was felt more by the front line staff than by policy makers and planners.

Staff who currently carry the responsibility for recruitment require expert advice from those with marketing skills, especially on how to develop recruitment strategies, how to address specific issues, and how to mount recruitment campaigns. Furthermore, carers will have to be involved at every stage, from policy to planning, recruitment, selection and training and be given a much more central role than at present. We had many comments suggesting that experienced carers are in a much better position (than placement staff) to address some of the fears and uncertainties of the public and some of the public's perceptions and stereotypes about the children and social workers. Besides carers, young people, too, who are in foster care or have experienced foster care, birth parents and the carers' own children should have a vital contribution to make in activities associated with recruitment, preparation and training.

The study found that successful recruitment processes are typically local (word of mouth and the local press), but some kind of national initiative and co-ordination with local authorities could make additional contributions by:

- making use of national media more effectively, notably TV;
- pooling resources and considering campaigns between authorities;
- sharing ideas and targeting strategies;
- obtaining advice on marketing;
- retaining the services of carers who move across administrative boundaries.

Recruitment campaigns and activities are expensive and labour intensive to mount. To avoid duplication, neighbouring authorities should be encouraged both in this and other similar activities (training, stand-by service) to pool resources and to co-ordinate their work. Such co-operation could also result in more placement sharing to respond to some highly specialised needs that a minority of children present and which cannot usually be provided by small authorities. Although the study has not found a blueprint for recruitment, the following qualities appear to aid recruitment and retention greatly (see also Appendix A):

• a good knowledge of the area and of the agency's fostering needs;
• having a well organised and responsive fostering service;
• having satisfied carers who are involved as partners;
• undertaking ongoing local recruitment campaigns;
• consistently involving carers and young people in recruitment, preparation and training;
• a high profile of the fostering service maintained by senior management and councillors;
• well thought-out financial arrangements, including payments to carers.
• maintaining continuity in recruitment.

Preparation and continued training for carers
Training received considerable praise from carers, but there was also a strong call for far more continued and systematic training to help enhance the carers' knowledge and skills. With over half the children referred for fostering placement presenting behavioural and emotional problems, carers were expecting to be equipped with more specific skills connected with the management of such behaviours and needs. Much more input was also expected in relation to children having a disability or health problem, issues on contact, and the emotional impact of fostering on carers and their families. Carers who felt prepared were less likely to say that they found the children more difficult than they expected or that they felt like giving up.

Chapter 6 highlighted the blurring of the stages and timing of family assessment, preparation, training, participation in support groups and continued training, calling for greater differentiation. It was far from clear where one stopped and another began. No doubt there are overlaps, but distinctiveness is also necessary. In this way training also begins to assume its importance and sets the scene for continued training. Overall, a more coherent, systematic and continued form of training was being

requested by carers with the possibility of it leading to higher qualifications for those who wanted them.

Without diluting the importance of separate training for carers, we
would also like to stress the necessity of periodic joint forms of training
for all those involved in the planning and delivery of services to
children. Besides helping to improve working relationships and reduce
existing stereotypes about each other, it could also help to promote
greater identification with the task and the agency as a whole. Some
authorities are already doing a fair amount in this direction, but far
more is needed.

A number of implications for policy and practice also arise from the
findings set out in Chapter 9 on children who foster. For example,
preparation, training and post-placement services could do much more
than at present to involve and take seriously the preparation and support
of the whole fostering family. So often the outcome of the placement
depends on the attitude of the fostering household's children. Both own
and foster children can carry many fears and anxieties which appear to
be underestimated by those around them. Even when children appear to
know, they do not also necessarily understand about what is happening
and its likely implications for themselves and others. Like the adults,
the children too need to be listened to, sounded out and prepared on
their readiness to foster, how to anticipate and deal with difficulties, and
how to handle sensitive background information. They need to be
prepared for children leaving, give them a higher profile in the agreement, and offer more concentrated support during and after the placement is ended.

There are also a number of other ways which could help reduce the
possibility of difficulties arising for both own and foster children. For
instance, careful assessment and matching are especially needed when
placing children who have been abused or having abused others, children
who have been badly rejected, or those who appear very needy for
attention. It is important to refrain from placing children of the same
age as that of an own child; this has been found by this and other studies
to carry significant risks. Similarly, avoid the placement of children
who are older than the carers' own by less than five years. The investment
in time for more detailed preparation, matching and support should be

made up by placements lasting as planned and carers continuing to foster for periods longer than the average of seven years found at present.

Role ambiguities and uncertainties

Role ambiguities, uncertainty about expectations, and some tensions appeared to surround the relationship between carers and children's social workers and that of child care area teams and of the placement service. These roles and relationships have always been difficult because of their complexity. It has not become any easier with the different types of fostering that have been introduced over the years and the more central role now expected of and often played by the children's parents. These developments have mainly resulted in more expectations being placed on both carers and social work staff. The introduction of a link worker into this equation, popular as it has proved with carers, has introduced a further possibility for confusion of roles and expectations and sometimes has given rise to divided loyalties. Perhaps unfairly, children's workers, because of the more controlling nature of their role, have sometimes been singled out for criticism.

We found uncertainty amongst many carers as to who carries overall responsibility for the child care plan and who is the first port of call when it comes to the need for support in relation to the child. Similar uncertainties and differences of opinion were also found amongst many service managers. Who does what is currently not clear and existing guidelines hedge the issue. Staff manuals examined were found to be vague, especially on the specific role of social workers in relation to the child and the foster carers. Because of this, and the unavailability at times of children's workers, carers made too many demands on link workers' time.

It was equally vague who was meant to act as the carers' first line manager and what the content of this role was seen to be. For example, would some of the carers' expectations for support be further met by the provision of a more structured form of supervision focusing on accountability, development and support? Contrary to the amount of literature surrounding the concept of supervision in social work, there is little or no reference to it in relation to carers and fostering and no agency made reference to this in relation to their carers.

How the two kinds of worker, including their managers and administrative staff, could complement each other in their work with the children and foster carers merits much more thought. As already mentioned, these two parts of the service currently operate at different levels of effectiveness. Besides responsibilities that should be laid on managers to promote better co-ordination, specific fostering agreements could be used to promote greater clarity and accountability. Some of the uncertainties, ambiguities and tensions found could be addressed by:

- clearer delineation of roles and clearer sign-posting of the areas of complementarity of the two types of worker;
- social workers having more time to spend with the children and their carers;
- more explanation and open sharing of differences and of different approaches especially to questions of discipline and control;
- carers being seen as members of the fostering team and involved in all decisions and planning concerning the children;
- social workers becoming more knowledgeable and skilled in fostering work and direct work with children;
- improved management;
- more joint training of staff and carers to help dispel some of the misunderstandings and stereotypes held about each other and which would contribute towards better team work.

The assessment and matching of children

The Census of supply and demand highlighted the scale of the assessment and matching task facing the fostering service. Over a 12 month period, the fostering placement services can expect around 8,000 referrals. In England, this would amount to almost 80,000 children referred annually. Over half of these are referred as emergencies requiring foster homes to be found urgently within a climate of scarcities. The Census survey further established that two-fifths of the children referred for placement were either not placed within the period of the Census and two weeks after, or placed in households which were not a first choice because of the non-availability of placements. We do not know how many more children were not referred because of the knowledge that the prospects of finding a placement were low, though anecdotal evidence indicates this happens.

Contrary to what the theoretical and research literature suggest should happen, most placements made were supply led rather than led by the children's needs (Triseliotis *et al*, 1995a and 1995b). When it came to balancing needs, preferences and placement availability, certain groups of children presented the placement services with big problems with many of these children remaining unplaced. Placements were badly needed for:

- children from minority ethnic groups;
- those requiring long-term placement;
- offenders;
- children with disabilities, especially learning difficulties;
- those displaying behavioural/emotional problems and school problems;
- older children.

It was even more difficult, apparently, to achieve matching in smaller authorities because there was only a very small pool of carers available and inter-authority placements proved more difficult to negotiate. Budget constraints made it difficult for authorities to access placements from the non-statutory sector.

Beyond these resource and supply considerations, concerns were also found about the process of assessment and matching. Clear guidelines appear to be needed on a range of issues relevant to matching, including the form of assessment that should precede placement requests and which children are meant to be matched and which not. The obscure divisions found between "planned" and "unplanned" or between "temporary", "permanent", "short-term", "long-term" and "emergency" placements, besides their inconsistency, disguised the need for the assessment and matching of a much larger group of children than currently undertaken.

Matching intentions featuring in some manuals were at odds with what was happening in practice. The absence also of updated information technology systems linking carers' characteristics, levels of skills and preferences with children's needs led to a significant number of placement decisions being made on very limited data. It was encouraging, as found in Chapter 7 that the majority of placed children went to first choice placements, but questions could still be asked about the very high proportion of children referred as emergencies (55 per cent). As a result, some children went to carers without proper assessment or sufficient background information, something carers resented.

Availability and support

Carers came into fostering because they were mostly motivated by the wish to do something for children in need and expected the service to have a similar commitment. In the majority of cases, the service was perceived by them to be responsive and there was a lot of praise, particularly for individual members of staff. When, however, the service was seen to fall short of a similar commitment and standard as their own, carers found this hard to comprehend and it forced them to question their decision to foster. It is in this context that a minority make the decision to leave. As a number of carers put it to us:

If they (agency/social workers) are not doing things for the children, they are not helping us.

Preparation before placement, training, and foster care manuals usually lead carers to expect support in the form of visits, availability, team work, problem-solving and responsiveness to crises over a 24 hour period. In most carers' views, all these aspects of service delivery constituted support, but it was not always forthcoming. Most complaints were about infrequent visits, cancelled visits, unavailability, unresponsiveness, not being listened to or understood, and lack of support to themselves and the children by children's social workers. The scarcity of specialist services for children, in the form of psychological and psychiatric help, was increasing the pressure on carers to find solutions to some children's complex problems. The limitations in knowledge and expertise of the standby service was also pointed out.

Because of the kind of children they are asked to care for, it was also the view of many carers that it was essential that the 24 hour standby general service should have at least one person present who is experienced in fostering work. Furthermore, because of dissatisfactions expressed by some carers with part-time staff, management needs to develop the kind of structures that ensure availability and continuity between full and part-time staff.

The authorities, too, were criticised for not listening more, for not being appreciative enough and for not making sufficient resources available for adequate support to be provided to the children and their carers. Even a majority of satisfied carers said that these were all areas about which authorities could do more about. Many of them commented on the increased demands on their time arising from having to attend meetings and reviews, visit schools and doctors, keep records, work with parents and promote contact, while confronting constant fears about false allegations of abuse.

It was exceptional for a manager to contradict the carers' views as outlined above. They acknowledged that looked after children did not receive, on the whole, the same attention and priority as "child protection" cases. A recurrent theme was that, when under pressure, children's workers were glad to simply have a "safe" place for the child, like a foster home.

The peripheral role of carers within the agency

The majority of carers are asked to care for and help some very vulnerable and sometimes troublesome children and they require more than recognition for what they are doing. They expect improved conditions of work and good training and team work to be made more of a reality. Yet their present status within authorities was found to be ambiguous and somewhat peripheral. They are neither members of staff nor exactly outsiders and feel that they have a low status within the organisation.

The official message, as it appears in manuals, is one of partnership, but this does not often match up with the reality of policy and practice. Partnership implies a redistribution of power with which authorities have yet to come to terms. Examples of partnership quoted by carers were few and this was confirmed by the authorities. Without diminishing the work of individual authorities and individual managers who have gone to great lengths to promote team work, carers largely perceived themselves as outsiders and of low status. Their current limited role in the planning and running of the fostering service largely reflected the ambivalent attitudes towards them held by authorities, reinforcing perceptions of themselves as being "second class" and of low status. Other experiences discussed earlier and under financial arrangements reinforced these feelings.

Carers appeared to be caught in a kind of double bind, that is, at times being seen as "paid professionals" who should be getting on with the job without needing support, and at other time being viewed as "amateurs" or "volunteers" who could not be trusted with information or with whom team work was not realistic. Overall, and not infrequently, a significant number of them came to feel isolated and alone.

Not surprisingly, perhaps, the carers' rapport with authorities as corporate bodies was found to be low. Their first identification was with the children, then their link workers, followed by the social worker and lastly the agency. They identified positively with individual members of staff rather than staff as representatives of the organisation. Increasing satisfaction and promoting greater identification between authorities and carers should also have a positive impact on recruitment and retention.

The carers and the children's parents
Some carers' commitment to the view that it is in most children's interests to have contact with their families was found to be rather weak. This could also explain the low proportion of contact visits that took place in the foster home. Carers and parents were sometimes physically set apart by the way contact is managed. This is not consistent with the thrust of the current legislation to promote continued parental responsibility and contact (unless contrary to the child's best interests). Neither is this consistent with research findings which demonstrate that continuing contact with parents, 'managed carefully by social workers where necessary', benefits the children and speeds up reunification (for a summary of the research evidence see Triseliotis, 1989; Berridge, 1997).

Most foster carers saw themselves as being "child-centred", i.e. that interest in children and/or a desire to help children were the key motivating factors that brought them into fostering. This means focusing on the individual child's well-being, often trying to restore their confidence and help them overcome painful and damaging experiences. Birth parents were sometimes blamed for their children's hardship which may make it difficult to include them in the restorative process. In our view, more consistent training and the carers' fuller participation in team work and ownership of the plan could promote greater commitment also to contact and restoration plans. The promotion of contact is as much a matter of planning as of attitudes. It has to feature more prominently in the care plans and agreements and be regularly monitored and reviewed.

Some manuals and managers made reference to carers working with the children's families, but with few exceptions the "how" of doing this had not been specified in writing. In interviews, some carers were uncertain of what this exactly meant and how it could be put into practice. An interesting example initiated by one agency in this direction, and referred to in Chapter 10, is worth exploring by other authorities. If wider expectations were to be placed on carers "to work with parents", then this needs to be supported by continued training, specified in care plans and in placement agreements, and reflected in levels of remuneration. It has also to be recognised, as a number of carers told us, that caring for the children left them with little time or energy to work with parents.

Assuring and controlling quality

In their pursuit of good quality practice, many authorities were trying to strike a balance between quality assurance measures to "guarantee" overall performance and avoid "disasters" through quality control. Ensuring that requirements and intentions are systematically observed, such as panels, reviews and inspections, is a skilled and labour intensive process. It requires proper resourcing, good organisation and efficient management. Unsurprisingly, perhaps, the systematic observation of existing arrangements, while mostly intended, was still some way from being achieved at the time of the study. This task was further hampered by the absence of suitable management information and monitoring systems.

So far the participation of key stakeholders such as children, young people, their families and carers in the planning, review and evaluation of the fostering service has been patchy.

Financial arrangements

A number of major financial matters emerged that local authorities, individually or collectively, have to consider as a matter of urgency because they generate much dissatisfaction and have an adverse impact on both recruitment and retention of carers as well as morale. Much greater confidence has to be restored amongst carers concerning the efficient management of their pay, whether in the form of allowances, fees or individual grants. The lack of attention apparently paid to their grievances by most of the former authorities, along with the perception of their being peripheral to the service, as described earlier, again conveyed to some carers feelings of being "second class" and perhaps not worthy of attention.

Many carers were also puzzled and perplexed by the multiplicity of payment systems operating within and between authorities and so were a number of managers. Some carers were themselves uncertain of which type of payment scheme they were on. It was for this reason that many of them and a number of managers were in favour of a national scheme which offered realistic pensionable payments, which was also seen to be consistent and fair.

Achieving a better payment system was hampered by serious budgetary constraints facing many authorities and negative attitudes held by some towards rewarding carers for their services, along with a failure to appreciate the position of the fostering service in present day society. This harbours dangers for the service. In spite of the fact that carers demonstrated high levels of commitment to their local authorities and to the care of local children, their loyalty could not be taken for granted. At the time of the study, the non-statutory sector was paying carers around three times more than the weekly fee paid by local authorities and making available more benefits and improved support packages.

Key policy recommendations

Specific policy issues requiring attention include the need to :
- Raise the image and profile of the fostering service within councils. A number of authorities have already made strenuous efforts to involve their councillors and top managers, including other services in the provision of child care and fostering services. This needs to become a standard practice.

- Develop up-to-date long-term fostering policies and planning strategies based on efficient management information systems.
- Make available sufficient resources to enable staff to engage in long-term recruitment, undertake more direct work with children, and provide more support services to foster carers.
- Adopt a more marketing oriented approach to recruitment, including the adoption of longer term strategies that recognise changing social, demographic and employment factors.
- Integrate the organisation, management and delivery of all placement services without jeopardising the distinctiveness of each, in order to create a highly specialised, knowledgeable and responsive service for all looked after children.
- Promote much greater teamwork and partnership between authorities and carers.
- Establish more adequate systems for obtaining feedback from all stakeholders in the service.
- Set in place consistent policies on the fostering of children by relatives.
- Develop adequate systems of management information to aid fostering policy making, long-term fostering strategies, planning, recruitment and the matching of children to carers.
- Respond to the financial aspirations of carers and set in place mechanisms for the efficient payment of allowances and grants to them. As a temporary step, the attachment of pension rights to fees and enhanced allowances could go some way in meeting the carers' aspirations.

Considering the small size of many authorities and limitations of their resources, it will be to their advantage to encourage much more sharing in such areas as recruitment, training, expertise, standby support, placement sharing, and the monitoring and evaluation of the service.

Some specific recommendations for managers
Senior management have the opportunity to address a number of issues arising from the study, including:
- Aiming for a single management structure for all services for looked

after children, including the integration of all these services, while generally safeguarding their distinctiveness.

- Clear statements about the respective roles of social worker and placement worker, especially in relation to decision-making, direct work with children, support to carers and the supervision of carers.
- Guidelines on the content of children's assessment and on the matching process. (Not surprisingly, perhaps, many staff are frustrated about the many different types of reports they have to produce on the same child. A more uniform approach is required, perhaps such as the ones suggested in the Looking After Children Schedules.)
- Improved co-ordination and communication between the various parts of the fostering service and especially between child care area teams and the placement service.
- The significant upgrading of the quality of the service currently provided to children in foster care and to foster carers by children's social workers to equal that offered by the placement part of the service.
- A 24 hour support service with staff who include one or more people who are knowledgeable about family placement issues.
- Aiming for greater continuity in children's social workers and using part-time staff in ways that ensure availability and continuity.
- Guidance to managers lower down the line on setting priorities, monitoring and managing in ways that ensure and control the quality of the service provided.
- The creation of lines of communication between carers' representatives and top management.
- Ensuring that all those working in foster care have the necessary training to undertake such work. It is unacceptable that many carers appear to have more understanding of fostering and of children's needs than many children's social workers.
- Increased forms of joint training involving staff from area teams, residential staff and carers.
- Aiming for more coherent forms of training and continued training for all carers, while also distinguishing more clearly between preparation, assessment, training, support groups and continued training.

The plethora of fostering terms currently used to describe what are essentially similar arrangements or types of need are confusing and can mask the extent of need. Agreement is required for a more consistent classification of carers and of fostering terms to facilitate the development of a common fostering language. Such a step should aid recruitment campaigns, provide clarity when assessing and matching children, avoid possible misunderstandings when arranging cross agency placements and agreements, and present policy makers and the public with a clearer view of what fostering is about.

Some key practice and training considerations

The majority of social workers working with children in foster care were providing an adequate and sometimes more than adequate service, but gaps remained. As a result, a significant number of carers had no confidence in the knowledge and expertise of their social workers to engage in problem-solving, when necessary. Some key requirements include:

- Acquiring far more knowledge and expertise, than at present, on child development, placement issues and fostering, and direct work with children.
- Getting to know better the children in foster care.
- Demonstrating greater responsiveness, appreciation of carers and greater reliability.
- Improving the quality of the assessment reports which are provided to placement staff for matching purposes.
- Working in partnership with carers, providing them with information on the children and sharing with them in problem-solving where necessary.
- Paying more attention to the foster carers' own children.
- Helping carers and their children manage feelings over the ending of placements.

Some considerations for national governments

The study points to a number of initiatives at national level, including:

- Outlining its own long-term strategy and resourcing of the fostering service.
- Encouraging and organising recruitment publicity through the national media.

- Providing advice on marketing skills to authorities that could help the recruitment of carers.
- Encouraging greater co-operation and sharing between authorities.
- Giving consideration to a national system for paying carers.
- The adoption of national foster care standards.

OVERVIEW

In final conclusion, the overall findings from the study suggest a service with many strengths. Much of the fostering work was permeated by a strong sense of commitment, along with a readiness to take risks and face challenges. Nevertheless, a number of key areas require much greater attention including:

- Developing long-term strategies on fostering.
- Adopting a marketing approach to recruitment.
- Moving towards the integration of services for all looked after children, and separating them from child protection work and emergencies.
- Improving methods of assessing and matching children to carers.
- Significantly improving the support services available to children and carers, especially those provided by social workers.
- Giving fuller expression to the concept of partnership with stakeholders.
- Responding to the aspirations of carers for team work, continued training and improved conditions of service.

The above recommendations have to be seen as a total package, rather than one to select from. Failing that, the local authority fostering service is likely to become more fragmented. Furthermore, an increasing proportion of the more difficult children and those with disabilities are likely to go to the non-statutory sector at much higher costs to local authorities. Worse, it could eventually lead to the disappearance of a local authority fostering service.

References

Adamson G (1973) *The Care-takers*, London: Bookstall Publications.

Aldgate J (1980) 'Identification of factors influencing children's length of stay in care', in Triseliotis J (ed) New *Developments in Foster Care and Adoption*, London: Routledge & Kegan Paul.

Aldgate J and Hawley D (1986) 'Helping foster families through disruption', *Adoption & Fostering*, 10:2, pp 44–49 & 58.

Ames I (1993) *We Have Learnt a Lot from Them: Foster care for young people with learning difficulties*, Barkingside: Barnardo's/National Children's Bureau.

Atherton C (1993) 'Reunification: Parallels between placement in new families and reunifying children with their families', in Marsh P and Triseliotis J (eds) *Prevention and Reunification in Child Care*, London: Batsford.

Audit Commission (1994) *Seen But Not Heard*, London: Audit Commission.

Barth R P and Berry M (1988) *Adoption and Disruption: Rates, risks and responses*, NY: Aldine de Gruyter, USA.

Bebbington A and Miles J (1990) 'The supply of foster families for children in care', *British Journal of Social Work*, 20:4, pp 283–307.

Berridge D and Cleaver H (1987) *Foster Home Breakdown*, Oxford: Blackwell.

Berridge D (1997) *Foster Care: A research review*, London: The Stationery Office.

Berridge D and Brodie I (1998) *Children's Homes Revisited*, Jessica Kingsley, London.

Brannen J (1992) *Mixing Methods: Qualitative and quantitative research*, Aldershot: Avebury.

Bullock R, Little M and Millham S (1993) *Going Home: The return of children separated from their families*, Aldershot: Gower.

Butler S and Charles M (1999) 'The past, the present, but never the future: Thematic representation of fostering disruption', *Child & Family Social Work*, 4:1, pp 9–20.

Caesar G, Parchment M and Berridge D (1994) *Black Perspectives on Services for Children in Need*, Barkingside: Barnardo's/National Children's Bureau.

Cambridgeshire County Council (1990) Social Services Department, *Consumer Survey: Foster carers*, Cambridgeshire County Council.

Campbell C and Whitelaw-Downs S (1987) 'The impact of economic incentives on foster parents', *Social Service Review*, 61:5, pp 99–60.

Caplan C (1988) 'The biological children of foster parents in the foster family', *Child and Adolescent Social Work*, 5:4, pp 281–299.

Chamberlain P, Moreland S and Reid K (1992) 'Enhanced services and stipends for foster parents: Effects on retention rates and outcomes for children', *Child Welfare*, 71:5, pp 38–41.

Cleaver H (1997) *Focus on Teenagers: Research into practice*, London: Department of Health.

Cleaver H (1997) 'Contact: the social workers' experience', *Adoption & Fostering*, 21:4, pp 34–40.

Cliffe D with Berridge D (1991) *Closing Children's Homes: An end to residential child care?* London: National Children's Bureau.

Coffin G (1993) *Changing Child Care: The Children Act 1989 and the Management of Change* (Birmingham Social Services Department), London: National Children's Bureau.

Dando I and Minty B (1987) 'What makes good foster parents', *British Institute of Social Work*, 17:3, pp 83–400.

Department of Health (1985) *Social Work Decisions in Child Care*, London: HMSO.

Department of Health (1991) *Patterns and Outcomes of placement*, London: DoH.

Department of Health (1995) Children *in Care in England and Wales, 1993*, Stanmore: DoH Leaflets.

Department of Health (1995) *Inspection of Local Authority Fostering Services*, Social Services Inspectorate, London: HMSO.

Downes C (1987) 'Fostered Teenagers and Children in the Family', *Adoption & Fostering*, 11:4, pp 11–18.

Fanshel D (1966) *Foster Parenthood*, University of Minnesota Press, USA.

Fletcher B (1993) *Not Just a Name: The views of young people in foster and residential care*, London: National Consumer Council and Who Cares? Trust.

Galbraith L (1991) *Foster care in Dundee: Public perceptions and carers views*, Dundee, Report to Tayside Regional Council.

George V (1970) *Foster Care: Theory and practice*, London: Routledge.

Gilchrist A and Hoggan P (1996) 'Involving birth parents in foster care training', *Adoption & Fostering*, 20:1, pp 30–34.

Gray P G and Parr E A (1957) *Children in Care and the Recruitment of Foster Parents*, London: Home Office.

Gregg P (1993) 'Why do Foster Parents Cease to Foster? A study of the perceptions of foster parents', M.Phil. thesis submitted to the University of Southampton.

Hill M, Lambert L and Triseliotis J (1989) *Achieving Adoption With Love and Money*, London: National Children's Bureau.

Holman R (1973) Trading *in Children*, London: Routledge & Kegan Paul.

Holman R (1980) Inclusive and Exclusive Concepts of Fostering, in Triseliotis J (ed.) *New Developments in Foster Care and Adoption*, London: Routledge & Kegan Paul.

House of Commons Health Committee (1998) Children *Looked After by Local Authorities*, Vol. I. London: HMSO.

Hutchinson D (1951) *In Quest for Foster Parents*, NY, Columbia University Press, USA.

Jenkins R (1969) 'Long-term fostering', *Case Conference, 15:9*.

Jenkins S and Norman E (1972) *Filial Deprivation and Foster Care*, NY, Columbia University Press, USA.

Jones A and Bilton K (1994) *The Future Shape of Children's Services*, London: National Children's Bureau.

Jones E O (1975) 'A study of those who cease to foster', *British Journal of Social Work*, 5:1, pp 31–41.

Keefe A (1983) *Foster Care: A research study on the NCH project in Gloucester and Avon*, London: National Children's Home.

Kent R (1997) *Children's Safeguards Reviews*, Edinburgh, Social Work Services Group.

Knapp M and Fenyo A (1989) *Efficiency in Foster Family Care: Proceeding with caution*, Canterbury, University of Kent, Personal Social Services Research Unit.

Kufeldt K, Armstrong J and Dorosh M (1989) 'In care, in contact?', in Hudson J and Galaway B (eds.) *The State as Parent*, Dordrecht: Kluwer.

Lowe M (1990) 'Will foster care survive the 1990s?' in National Foster Care Association, *Foster Care for a Decade*, London: NFCA.

Lowe N, Murch M, Borkowski A, Beckford V with Thomas C (1999) *Supporting Adoption: Reframing the approach*, London: BAAF.

Martin G (1993) 'Foster care: The protection and training of carers' children', *Child Abuse Review*, 2, pp 15–22.

McAuley C (1996) *Children in Long Term Fostering*, Aldershot: Avebury.

Millham S, Bullock R, Hosie K and Haak M (1986) *Lost in Care*, Aldershot: Gower.

Minnis H (1999) *Results of the Foster Carers' Training Project*, Pamphlet, Glasgow.

Mullender A (ed.) (1999) *We are Family: Sibling relationships in placement and beyong*, London: BAAF.

National Foster Care Association (1997) *Foster Care in Crisis*, London: NFCA.

National Foster Care Association (1999) *UK National Standards for Foster Care*, London: NFCA.

Oldfield N (1997) *The Adequacy of Foster Care Allowances*, Aldershot: Ashgate.

Orkney Inquiry (1992) *The Report of the Inquiry into the Removal of Children from Orkney in February 1991.* Edinburgh: HMSO.

Pasztor E M and Wynne S F (1995) *Foster Parent Retention and Recruitment: The state of the art in practice and policy,* Washington DC: Child Welfare League of America, USA.

Parker R (1966) *Decision in Child Care,* London: Allen & Unwin.

Parker R (1978) 'Foster care in context', *Adoption & Fostering,* 2, pp 27–32.

Parker R (1999) *Adoption Now: Messages from research,* London: Wiley.

Part D (1993) 'Fostering as seen by the carers' children', *Adoption & Fostering,* 17:1, pp 26–30.

Pithouse A, Young C and Butler I (1994) *All Wales Review: Local Authority Fostering Services,* School of Social and Administrative Studies, Cardiff Law School, University of Wales.

Poland D and Groze V (1993) 'Effects of foster care placement on biological children in the home' *Child and Adolescent Social Work Journal,* 10:2, pp 153–164.

Pugh G (1996) 'Seen but not heard: addressing the needs of children who foster', *Adoption & Fostering,* 20:1, pp 3–41.

Quinton D, Rushton A, Dance C and Mayes D (1997) *Establishing Permanent Placements in Middle Childhood,* Chichester: Wiley.

Ramsay D (1996) 'Recruiting and retaining foster carers', *Adoption & Fostering,* 20:1, pp 42–46.

Reed J (1993) *We Have Learnt a Lot from Them: Foster care for young people with learning difficulties,* Barkingside: Barnardo's/National Children's Bureau.

Rhodes P (1993) 'Charitable vocation or proper job?' *Adoption & Fostering,* 17:1, pp 8–13.

Richards S (1999) 'LAC placement patterns: Managing the process', *Adoption & Fostering,* 22:4, pp 24–29.

Rowe J, Cain H, Hundleby M and Keane (1984) *Long-term Foster Care,* London: Batsford.

Rowe J, Cain H, Hundleby M and Garnett L (1989) *Child Care Now: A survey of placement patterns*, London: BAAF.

Sellick C (1992) *Supporting Short Term Foster Carers*, Aldershot: Avebury.

Sellick C and Thoburn I (1996) *What Works in Family Placement?* Barkingside: Barnardo's.

Shaw M and Hipgrave T (1989) 'Specialist fostering 1988 – a research study', *Adoption & Fostering*, 13:3, pp 17–21.

Simon L J (1975) 'The effect of foster-care payment levels on the number of foster children given homes', in *Social Services Review*, No. 49, September.

Sinclair R (1984) *Decision Making in Statutory Reviews on Children in Care*, Aldershot: Gower.

Sinclair R, Garnett L and Berridge D (1995) *Social Work and Assessment with Adolescents*, London: NCB.

Social Trends (1995) Central Statistical Office, London: HMSO.

Social Trends (1996) Central Statistical Office, London: HMSO.

Social Work Services Group (1996) *Scotland's Children: The Children (Scotland) Act 1995 Regulations and Guidance. Volume 2, Children Looked After by Local Authorities*, Edinburgh: Scottish Office.

Stone N M and Stone S F (1983) 'The prediction of successful foster placement', *Social Casework*, 64:1, pp 11–17.

Strathclyde Regional Council (1988) *Fostering and Adoption Disruptions: A preliminary study*, Glasgow, Strathclyde Regional Council, Social Work Department.

Strathclyde Regional Council (1991) 'The Outcome of Permanent Family Placement', in Scottish Office, *Adoption & Fostering*, Edinburgh: Scottish Office.

Thomas C and Beckford V with Lowe N and Murch M (1999) *Adopted Children Speaking*, London: BAAF.

Thorpe R (1974) *The Social and Psychological Situation of the Long-term Foster Child with Regard to his Natural Family*, PhD thesis, Nottingham University.

Trasler G (1960) *In Place of Parents.*, London: Routledge & Kegan Paul.

Triseliotis J (1973) *In Search of Origins*, London: Routledge & Kegan Paul.

Triseliotis J (ed.) (1980) *New Developments in Foster Care and Adoption*, London: Routledge & Kegan Paul.

Triseliotis J (ed.) (1988) *Groupwork in Adoption and Foster Care*, London: Batsford.

Triseliotis J (1989) 'Foster care outcomes: A review of key research findings', Adoption & *Fostering*, 13:3, pp 5–17.

Triseliotis J, Sellick C and Short R (1995a) *Foster Care: Theory and practice*, London: Batsford.

Triseliotis J, Borland M, Hill M and Lambert L (1995b) *Teenagers and the Social Work Services*, London: HMSO.

Triseliotis J, Borland M and Hill M (1999) *Fostering Good Relations: A study of foster care and foster carers in Scotland*, Edinburgh: The Scottish Office: 1998 and Part II.

Utting W (1997) *People Like Us: The report of the review of the safeguards for children living away from home*, London: The Stationery Office.

Vernon J and Fruin D (1986) *In Care: A study of social work decision making*, London: NCB.

Von A I (1988) *Fostering Adolescents – Effects on the host children*, M.Sc. Dissertation, Oxford University.

Waterhouse S (1992) 'How foster carers view contact', *Adoption & Fostering*, 16:2, pp 42–46.

Waterhouse S (1997) *The Organisation of Fostering Services*, London: NFCA.

Weinstein E A (1960) *The Self-image of the Foster Child*, NY, Russell Sage Foundation, USA.

Wilkinson C (1988) *Prospect, Process and Outcome in Foster Care*, M. Phil. thesis, Edinburgh University.

Wolkind S and Rushton A (1994) 'Residential and foster family care', in Rutter M, Taylor E, and Hersov E, (eds.) *Child and Adolescent Psychiatry: Modern approaches*, Oxford: Blackwell.

APPENDIX A

RECRUITMENT STRATEGIES SUGGESTED

Each authority is asked to consider which of the following recommendations apply to its own needs and circumstances.

Specific suggestions

- Local authorities, preferably collectively, will need to get professional advice on how to organise and promote fostering need and fostering campaigns. On the basis of what carers have said, a balance has to be struck between projecting children's needs and the job of fostering.

- Authorities should identify first what their exact foster care needs are, that is, what kind of children they have requiring foster homes, their age, possible behavioural and/or emotional difficulties, learning or other disabilities, racial and/or ethnic and cultural background and the kind of foster homes that would be needed to fit with these children's needs.

- Each authority will need to study both the profile of its existing carers as well as the population and other characteristics of their area, such as age composition, housing, employment patterns, especially for women, before deciding how and who to target.

- Give carers a central role and a much higher profile than at present, in all aspects of recruitment, preparation and training. Carers, young people with experience of fostering, carers' own children and birth parents can convey greater confidence and provide valued and accurate information helping to dispel stereotypes. They can also instil confidence in many people who are uncertain about putting themselves forward.

- One lesson to emerge from the research is that target groups have to be varied to take account of the specific area where the campaign is taking place. For example, in some of the rural areas more emphasis